FIFTY YEARS

ON THE

LONDON & NORTH WESTERN RAILWAY,

AND OTHER MEMORANDA

IN THE

LIFE OF DAVID STEVENSON.

EDITED BY LEOPOLD TURNER.

LONDON:
PRINTED BY McCORQUODALE & CO. LIMITED,
CARDINGTON STREET, EUSTON, N.W.

1891.

Transportation
Library
TF
140
.S85
A3

EDITOR'S PREFACE.

THESE writings have been placed in my hands for the purpose of submitting them to the public. I have found little to advise or suggest respecting them; my principal share in their introduction consisting of the addition to the sketch and letters of a few of Mr. Stevenson's poetical pieces—pieces which may, I think, enhance the interest the friends he already possesses are likely to take in the leading portion of his little work, and which may not, I trust, escape the approbation of those other friends whose companionship—granting it is to be enjoyed—must date from the day of publication.

L.T.

PREFACE.

IN the early days of my active service upon the railway, it was my practice to write almost daily, in easy journalistic fashion, to my dear friend and connection, the Rev. Robert Turnbull, Vicar of Wybunbury, Cheshire. He preserved some of the letters, and, at his lamented death, his widow returned them to me. A few friends requested me to write an introduction to them, giving some further account of my experience and recollection, and to publish them. With many misgivings as to the favourable acceptance of such lucubrations from me, even by the large body of railway men to whom my name is familiar, I consented to do so, reserving their publication until the period of my retirement from the service. The recollections were written long before the Jubilee Year, and the teeming personal accounts which then became the rage, and have since continued to flood the press, destroyed the little hope I ever had that my poor book would ever be of any general interest. It may, however, serve to recall my name to those railway friends and others, with whom for so many years my life has been passed, "when my place shall know me no more," and when for me at least, in all mundane considerations, the "pleasures of hope" shall have given place to the "pleasures of memory."

D.S.

CHAPTER I.

IN the leafy month of June, 1837, when the heralds were proclaiming the Princess Victoria queen of these realms, one of the most humble and loyal of her future subjects entered the service of the new method of locomotion called the Railway. That child of scientific invention had just begun to stretch its powerful limbs over the length and breadth of the land, and was destined to be one of the greatest influences towards the prosperity and progress of the good Queen's long and brilliant reign.

I was introduced to Mr. Ashlin Bagster, who had been appointed, at the nomination of Mr. Robert Stephenson, to be the first manager of the London and Birmingham line: a tall and serious-looking gentleman, who shook his head when, at his bidding, I copied a letter as a specimen of my hand-writing. I was, however, appointed a cadet in his office at a salary of twenty pounds per annum; the first clerk to the first manager of the railway!

It was an exciting period; for after a long and animated struggle, Mr. George Carr Glyn, the chairman, and his colleagues, had obtained the sanction of the legislature; Mr. Robert Stephenson had overcome the difficulties of surveying the line, at the point of the pitch-fork and other obstructions of the land-owners; had conquered the engineering difficulties, and nearly completed the work which a pamphleteer of the time endeavoured to prove to be a greater work than the erection of the Egyptian pyramids. The time had arrived when a portion of the line was to be opened to the public. The engines were ready, Mr. Joseph Wright's carriages were built, the stations were constructed as far as Boxmoor, twenty-three miles, and it was decided to engage the staff—clerks, porters, policemen, drivers, firemen, and mechanics

—and begin. Mr. Richard Creed and Captain Constantine Richard Moorsom were the joint secretaries prior to the opening of the railway. Mr. Creed had his office at Cornhill, in London, and Captain Moorsom at Birmingham. They were appointed in September, 1833. At the same time Robert Stephenson was selected as the engineer. This was at the first meeting of the Board. Previously the business of the Company had been conducted by two committees, one in London, and the other in Birmingham. Mr. Creed had been a partner in the banking house of Fauntleroy & Co., the head of which firm was executed for forgery, the last victim to the inhuman law in such cases. Mr. Creed had subsequently been sent by the Government to Paris to settle the English claims upon France consequent upon the Treaty of Peace.

The details of the preparation for the opening fell upon Mr. Bagster, at a salary of £400 per annum, and his small band of assistants at Euston, at salaries from £20 to £150. This gentleman provided many of the methods and forms which were adopted afterwards by most of the railways, and which still remain in use. Of those who took part in the preparations only a few rose to distinction in the development of railways. Mr. Bagster left the London and Birmingham, and took service on a northern line, but died early. Mr. Fox, the resident engineer, went into trade, and was knighted during the Exhibition of 1851. Mr. Kenneth Morison became the founder of the Railway Clearing House, and the remainder, disappearing in the course of time, made, as I have said, no mark of importance. Joseph Atkinson, the chief of the mechanics, whose father had been a near neighbour of the elder Stephenson in his humble days, was an ingenious inventor, and the author of the carriage truck still in use, and of improvements in waggons and other valuable aids to the new system. Ill health afterwards shortened his career of usefulness.

CHAPTER II.

ON the twentieth of July, 1837, the road to Boxmoor was opened by the Directors and their friends, and the down journey was conducted satisfactorily; but on the return, on descending the incline to Euston, the first of the two trains ran into collision with the end of the platform. The brakesman, Kirkup by name, turned the brake, which then worked from a seat on the top of the carriage, the wrong way, and lost command of the train. Kirkup gave an explanation in the broad Newcastle dialect, but as he was very much excited, I am unable to record it. The manager who was also inclined to Newcastle speech, said it was "pweposterwous." Plaster for broken heads, and a few repairs, soon restored matters, and the running of trains for the public commenced.

The following is a copy of the notice issued to the Public:—

LONDON AND BIRMINGHAM RAILWAY.

PARTIAL OPENING OF THE LINE, 1837.

The public are informed that on and after Thursday, the 20th inst., the Railway will be opened for the conveyance of Passengers and Parcels to and from London and Boxmoor, including the intermediate stations of Harrow and Watford.

First class coaches carry six passengers inside, and each seat is numbered.

Second class coaches carry eight passengers inside, and are covered, but without lining, cushions or divisions, and the seats are not numbered.

Third class coaches carry four passengers on each seat, and are without covering.

The following, until further notice, will be the times for departure of the Trains. On every day except Sundays.

First Time Bill of the London and Birmingham Railway, copied from Original.

London & Birmingham
RAILWAY.
1837.

HOURS OF DEPARTURE.

From London:

FIRST TRAIN	10 o'Clock.
SECOND do.	2 ,,
THIRD do.	5 ,,

From Boxmoor:

FIRST TRAIN	8 o'Clock.
SECOND do.	2 ,,
THIRD do.	7 ,,

ON SUNDAYS.

From London:

FIRST TRAIN	9 o'Clock.
SECOND do.	5 ,,
THIRD do.	7 ,,

From Boxmoor:

FIRST TRAIN	9 o'Clock.
SECOND do.	5 ,,
THIRD do.	7 ,,

Curiosity brought thousands of passengers; but in the third class open carriages the dust from the roofs of the tunnels and the newly made line, and the hot cinders from the engines, gave them rough travelling. Paper tickets were used torn from books with a reserved duplicate; and as the line opened to longer distances the name of each passenger booked was entered in the duplicate, after the manner of the old coaching days. On October 16th, 1837, the line was further opened to Tring, and on April 9th, to Denbigh Hall. The stage coaches and mails were conveyed on carriage-trucks to Denbigh Hall, thence by road to Rugby, and the rest of the journey by rail to Birmingham. The stations were enlivened by the sound of the bugle, but the coach-guards were disgusted with their outside ride on the railway. The railway guards also had an unpleasant time, for, adhering to old usage they too rode outside on the top of the carriage, where, amidst other disagreeables, their clothes sometimes caught fire. The roadside stations were enclosed with lofty iron railings, within which the passengers were imprisoned until the train arrived; they were then permitted to rush out to take their places, for which they sometimes had to join in a free fight. Then the engine gave a prolonged whistle, which Charles Dickens described as saying "Here are two hundred and fifty people in the veriest extremity of danger; and here are their two hundred and fifty screams all in one"! The clatter caused by the stone blocks, which were used before the wooden sleepers replaced them, added to the unpleasantness of the journey. Thus the success of the new mode of conveyance was not then established in the popular mind; and coach proprietors and others interested in its expected failure, still hoped on, and in many cases lost money by their lingering belief in the old system. Not so the leading men connected with the London establishment. Benjamin Worthy Horne, William Chaplin, and others, took early steps to connect themselves with the railway companies.

Horne and Chaplin became the London and Birmingham Co.'s agents for parcels and omnibuses, and did good service for many years in the organisation of branch coaches and in providing temporary conveyances in periods of floods and landslips when parts of the line became impassable. It was, however, some time before the general public fully believed in the permanence of the railways. Large sums were spent in improving the high roads for the coaches when the railways were approaching completion, and some were actually open for traffic.

CHAPTER III.

BY this time, near the site of the place where Trevithick had exhibited his first locomotive engine, Philip Hardwick's great Doric entrance to Euston reared its solid front, and was considered a handsome addition to the architecture of London. In removing the scaffolding, but fortunately while the men were at dinner, a large portion of the hugh baulks of timber, of which the scaffolding was composed, fell to the ground with a loud report.

In September, 1838, the line was opened throughout from London to Birmingham, and the duties of the several departments had become more defined. At first everybody made himself useful in that which came to hand. I collected cash bags from the stations, worked in the office, carried a torch at night when the trains were late—for we had no gas in the earlier months—booked passengers, engaged policemen or porters, and did anything else I was told. Sometimes I acted as brakesman to the passenger trains from Camden to Euston; and when the first Napoleon's celebrated general, Marshal Soult, paid us the honour of a visit, I assisted the General Manager and the Superintendent of Police in lowering the train to Euston, ordinary brakesmen being put aside on so important an occasion. Railway Managers of this day would be shocked at the free-and-easy use of the main line between Camden and Euston at this time. Thus, the manager rode to Euston on a waggon which he lowered himself; and any superior officer had the power to adopt this method of making the journey, quite regardless of what might be in the way. On one occasion, on taking down a very high-sided waggon, I had to stand outside the vehicle on the buffer, intending to work the brake with my foot, but midway I found I could not reach it, and I was only saved by the aid of a very long porter who happened to be with me. All hands were proficient at this braking, for we used to make small wagers as to stopping the waggons or carriages to an inch on the turntable at the bottom.

After serving a few months in the audit office, and in the opening of the through line to Birmingham, I was drafted from the Manager's office to Camden Station, in connection 1838. with the Stores and Construction Departments. This was a change for the worse as regards my personal comfort. The office was a rough wooden erection, with an earthen floor, and contained, by day, myself in my great coat, the stores of all kinds, a table, a small cabin stove, and the mice. Chalk Farm was in the country then, and I had to prepare my meals at the small stove, and to consume them assisted by the mice, who evidently had a great contempt for my presence. The place was always muddy. The station had been raised from the road by the earth from the Primrose Hill Tunnel, and this new clay produced a Slough of Despond, which I have only seen equalled at the Royal Agricultural Show, at Kilburn, a few years ago.

Still the building of waggons for the intended goods traffic went on, and I kept my books and blew my fingers until better times came. During this period I was instructed to obtain a sight of the patent for Booth's Patent Grease, some trouble having been experienced for want of a suitable lubricant for the carriage axles. I did so, and made the first can of the compound in my shed, and, as it was found successful, the Company afterwards purchased the use of the patent, and have adopted it ever since.

Chalk Farm Tavern was then at the end of a lane near my office. It had been, as is well known, a celebrated duelling place, and it still retained some of its faded grandeur, as a place of resort for dancing and *fêtes*. The large ball-room was decked with chandeliers and convex mirrors. An elevated gallery led to the tea-garden, at the entrance to which the figures of two soldiers were painted. The Chalk Farm Fair had not yet begun, but the navvies, during the making of the tunnel, had lowered the character of the place. When over their beer at night, their singing could be heard far away. A favourite chorus of theirs was to this effect:

"And the guns shall be rattling,
A-rattling and roaring,
A-rattling and roaring, Oho-o-o-o!"

The stentorian sound must have surprised the crows at Hampstead.

These navvies became quite a class when canals were cut, and came in valuably for the railway work. They took their designation from the word 'navigation,' and retained it after they had changed their occupation. The pure air and hard earth-work made them models of physique. They were utterly fearless, and were very fond of beer and an occasional fight, but were otherwise simple and honest fellows. They were in the habit of calling "Ware out," when anything was thrown down or falling; and it is said that a man, falling over his barrow at the mouth of an abyss, finding that he must inevitably fall down the shaft, cried, "Ware out! Navvie a-coming!" I do not, however, vouch for the truth of the story.

As a number of rats joined the mice and me in our shed, and the rain began to damage the books and goods, it was found necessary to make room for me in the office of the engineer and timekeepers, beneath an arch of Chalk Farm Bridge; and then we organised a daily ordinary at the Chalk Farm Tavern, which suited me better than the cabin-stove feasts. The wag of the party was our engineer, who ultimately became the General Manager of more than one important railway. He used to resent the bad fare provided for us, and played the old landlord many a practical joke. On one occasion a putrid sucking pig was served, and, as we could not eat it, our friend nailed it over the mantel-piece of the room and rang the bell. Boniface appeared and tore down the pig, anathematising us all. Pigeon-shooting at the place gave us pigeon-pies to satiety; but I suppose the pies were running short one day, when a lady and gentleman drove up and ordered dinner. The landlord came into our room and asked if we could spare the pie. We replied, "In a minute or two;" and it was then taken away, but not before "George" had abstracted the pigeons and replaced them with potatoes. "Guess," said he, "there will be a ringing of bells presently," and so there was; also the ordering of the horse and gig, in great indignation, and the departure of the lady and gentleman. At another time the cook was overheard remonstrating with the landlord on the unfitness of a goose for human food, when mine host was heard to say, "Oh, bless it, pepper it; pepper it; *they'll* eat it!" But that goose disappeared, and it has not yet been discovered what became of it.

CHAPTER IV.

THE working of the line went struggling towards a state of order. The rails were found to be too light for the traffic—56th fish-bellied rails in some cases—the stone blocks a failure; fires to luggage on the tops of the carriages frequent; signals by flag and hand lamps insufficient. The signalmen, dressed in police uniform, had been drilled by Mr. Superintendent Bedford, formerly of the Guards and lately of the Metropolitan Police, and they brought the flag-staff round to the shoulder, as the trains passed, with true military precision. But they were not enough, and signal posts were contemplated. These and many other defects occupied the Board and Management. The subject of goods traffic engaged much consideration, and, on the resignation of Mr. Bagster, Mr. Joseph Baxendale was appointed manager of the line. He removed the manager's office to Camden Station, in a building originally intended for the passenger booking office, before the extension of the railway to Euston. Into this building Mr. Robert Stephenson's office was also transferred, from a house in St. John's Wood, since called the Eyre Arms Tavern, in the grounds at the back of which the ladies and gentlemen used to practice for the celebrated Eglinton Tournament, which took place about this time. I am afraid they hindered the work of the drawing clerks very much, and for my own part I must confess that I sometimes tilted when I should have been otherwise engaged.

The stores and engineer's departments were likewise brought into the manager's building.

Two more suitable men could not have been called to the councils of the Board at such a period than Mr. Joseph Baxendale and Mr. Benjamin Worthy Horne. Their experience and energy, in relation to the conveyance both of passengers and goods, were of the highest order. Yet they were totally different in character, as in appearance. Mr. Horne was a tall wiry man, of determined face and rapid speech, quick in manner, irritable, and prompt of action. He largely contributed to the great efficiency of the stage coaches, and had been found a bitter opponent to many a competitor in the struggles for ascendancy on many a road. He once pointed out to me a road-side inn where he went one night, years before, and bought up all the horses of the coach opposed to his, driving by triumphantly in the morning where the rival coach, with its passengers, had come to an unexpected stand. Mr. Baxendale was a shorter and a broader man than Mr. Horne. He was cheerful and witty in conversation, ever had a word of encouragement for the youngsters, and was universally beloved by those whom he employed. The success of Pickford & Co., and the general efficiency of that establishment, proved his administrative power; and his foresight and wisdom at this critical time for carriers were borne out by eminent results. His clear system of forms and arrangements, by which a hold of the goods conveyed is maintained from the time they leave the consignor until they reach their destination, continues to be the basis of the carrying business all over the kingdom.

CHAPTER V.

THE goods traffic was commenced by the transfer of some of Messrs. Pickford & Co.'s extensive canal traffic to the line, and a small temporary loading shed was built for the purpose, in 1839. The old waggon sheds were removed, and an adequate workshop for the construction of waggons was erected; while at Euston a commodious carriage shop was established, the works being placed under Mr. Worsdell and his son.

1839

The endless rope by which the trains had been drawn up the incline from Euston was abolished, and the marine engines and two lofty chimneys at Camden were removed. The long discussed question of the adhesion of the locomotive engine wheels to the rails, had been settled in some degree, and that power had replaced the rope. The latter had long worked unsatisfactorily, causing many minor accidents, and on one occasion nearly destroying the writer of this humble record. The skid which was placed in the rear of the trains sometimes became partly detached, and was thrown about wildly on its passage up the incline, to the great alarm of persons walking on the line, of whom there were many at that time. The messenger rope from the foremost carriage to the endless rope frequently slipped or broke. The signal apparatus, which was a vessel on the principle of a gasometer, and moved some coloured water in a tube at the engine-house end, and also blew a whistle, failed occasionally.

Messrs. Cook and Wheatstone brought to the carriage shops a mysterious quantity of wire and began a series of electric experiments. Many wondrous reports were told us of our being likely to talk with people at a distance, by means of a wire and a pianoforte like instrument. There, in a corner of the carpenter's shop, reposed the embryo Puck, which was to put a girdle round the earth, remove prejudices, equalise prices, annihilate space, and, with its elder brother, the railway, mingle the races of men and become the many-leagued boots on the feet of Civilisation. But the doubting world received this invention with incredulity, as it ever does the boons which science confers.

On July 25th, 1837, two copper wires were laid between Euston and Camden, and the two quiet inventors placed themseves one at either end and conversed. The mighty and mysterious thing was proved a practical success, whose development would bring the human voice within instantaneous communication with each other at any distance, and make the whole world kin.

1837.

The gradual opening of Railways into London and other parts of the Kingdom brought us many learners of our forms and system, and occasionally we were sent to them to render assistance. On a trip of the kind to Leicester, I first met Mr. James Allport, of the Midland Railway, who was then doing duty in the booking office, from whence he rose to the rank of Director and Knighthood.

Further steps were taken to improve the goods traffic. A Goods Committee of Directors, with Captain Moorson for Chairman, was appointed; that gentleman having become a Director. Hitherto the Directors had not taken an active part in the details of the departments, and the power for the general management rested with the Chief Officers, their proceedings being confirmed by the Board in almost a merely formal way. The Chairman, Mr. Glyn, and his colleagues, confined their personal efforts to matters of policy, finance, &c. The Secretary was the Chief Officer, the Superintendent being responsible to him for the working and staff arrangements. Captain Moorsom, in his new office, began a more active control in the details of the young Goods Department. Mr. Wyatt, from Pickford & Co's establishment, was made the Goods Manager, and the Company began to carry on toll for some of the important carriers, in addition to Pickford and Co. Mr. Baxendale, at this time, resigned the superintendence of the line, and was succeeded by Mr. H. P. Bruyeres, a late Officer of Engineers. The goods traffic progressed but slowly, however, although inducements were offered to road and canal carriers to transfer their business to the railway.

At this time I volunteered from the Stores into the Goods Department, which had always seemed to me the most interesting and important branch of the business. I had already familiarised myself with the parcels work, in my leisure evenings, and I made the change, believing that the merchandise branch of the railways would afford the best career, although I knew it to be the most difficult and arduous.

1840.

After a few years' service Mr. Wyatt died, and was succeeded by Mr. Thomas C. Mills, formerly connected with the Birmingham Coaches, and subsequently Station Master at Birmingham. He had exhibited considerable energy during the riots at Birmingham, when the Company's station was threatened. In appearance he resembled the representations of Oliver Cromwell. He had much of that great man's bluntness of character, without, I fear, much of his piety. Under his management the tolls were so considerably reduced as to command the bulk of the general trade hitherto sent by canal. Sheds were erected for the large carriers, for which they paid a rental; and Pickford & Co. built their own premises, adjoining the station, on land purchased by Mr. Baxendale years before, in anticipation. Chaplin & Horne became Goods agents for the Grand Junction Railway Co., and had also suitable accommodation provided for them at Camden. The Company provided waggons which they placed in a siding, from whence the carriers turned them into their respective sheds. Occasionally the Company supplied tarpaulins for the waggons, for which a charge was made. I am precise in stating this arrangement, because of attempts in after years to deny the rights of Railway Companies to terminal charges. When the legislature first provided for the toll upon Turnpike Roads, the term did not include any services but the transit over the roadway; the coach proprietors and others using the way provided their own terminal conveniences.' We find the term "toll" used again in reference to the Canal charges; and here also the carriers were permitted to use the water-way for the toll they paid, and provide their own quays, wharves, and warehouses at the end of the journey. Pickford & Co. built their terminal at the City Basin; and others rented wharves. It is reasonable to suppose that when the Parliamentary powers were granted to the railways, the repetition of the use of this word "toll" was intended to convey the same meaning as when it was used by the same powers for canals and roadways. Mr. Baxendale, the largest carrier at the time, certainly expected that any future carrier on toll upon the railway would have to rent or provide his own terminal conveniences, in addition to the payment of the toll for the use of the line. Some years before the London railways carried any goods, Mr. Baxendale took the opportunity of purchasing land adjoining the London and North Western Railway at Camden Station, as before mentioned, sufficient to receive his warehouses when the time should come for the transfer of his traffic from the canal to the railway. On this piece of ground he afterwards erected his premises at Camden Station, and carried on the trade of carrier on toll; while his competitors rented sheds, cranes, &c., within the station, which were built by the Railway Company. Thus, it was thoroughly understood at this period that the toll did not include the terminals; and I think the fact fully shows that the attempt to force the Companies to provide costly stations, and then to deprive them of the right to a fair remuneration for the provision, was altogether unjust, and contrary to all originally understood notions on the subject.

Under the altered system the traffic increased week by week. It fell to my duty to make up the daily totals from the weights of the Company, dividing it under the several rates 1844. according to the declarations of the carriers; a severe task, for many hours each day. I, however, held out, and received gratifying promotion. The staff were gradually increased, and my position grew in importance. We discovered that the declarations of some of the carriers as to the description of goods loaded by them in the waggons were often systematically false, and we had to appoint a detective, who frequently found the real invoices in the waggons to differ entirely from the declarations given to the Company. It also happened that when trade was brisk, and waggons were in large demand, the carriers' men would have a pitched battle for the vehicles; it was also found that loads made up at country stations, where the weight could not be checked, were overloaded to a dangerous extent.

Meanwhile the higher authorities were commencing negotiations for amalgamating the London and Birmingham, the Grand Junction, and the Manchester and Birmingham Railways into a line to be called the London and North Western Railway, under one corporation. The Act of Parliament confirming the amalgamation was passed on July 16th, 1846, after a long series of jealousies and unworthy squabblings.

Mr. Glyn became the Chairman of the new Company, Robert Stephenson was made the engineer-in-chief of the amalgamated Companies in 1844, but the London and North Western Railway was not in full operation until 1851. The engineering duties were divided into sections; Mr. R. B. Dockray taking the Southern Division, Mr. Norris and others the Northern section. After 1851, Mr. Stephenson had only a consulting fee. Captain Mark Huish came to London from Liverpool, and was installed as General Manager; which was announced by a flourish of trumpets in the form of a circular. His salary was fixed at £2,000 per annum; calling for much comment, as a monstrous stipend: one writer declaring that no manager could be worth such a salary.

Mr. Glyn was well entitled to his increased dignity. He was an enlightened gentleman, and his services towards the development of railways were afterwards deservedly recognised by his elevation to the peerage, under the title of Lord Wolverton in the choice of which name he paid a graceful compliment to the locomotive centre of the London and Birmingham line, and the station where her Majesty passed the night on one of her earliest railway journeys.

Captain Huish was a man of stern demeanour in business. He managed the line from his office, seldom visiting the stations, but left the details almost wholly in the hands of his responsible officers. In private life he was a genial gentleman, a warm friend, and ever ready to promote any enterprise for the moral and material improvement of the poor. He was possessed of considerable literary power, and wrote more than one talented paper on the condition and prospects of the railway. After his retirement he resided at Bonchurch, where his active benevolence rendered him generally respected. On his monument in the Bonchurch graveyard his former connection with the Bengal native infantry is recorded, but no mention is made of his distinguished position with the greatest of English railways.

So ended the London and Birmingham Railway Company as a distinct body; a happy family of directors and servants, every one of whom deemed it an honour to be connected with the development of the new mode of locomotion. The directors were generous and considerate to their officers and servants, and the managers worthily interpreted the intentions of the directors towards the rank and file. Censure was applied in a manner to convince the delinquent of the justice of a rebuke, while judicious praise stimulated the exertions of good workers. The establishment being within reasonable compass, the subsequent modern dogmatic and unreasoning discipline was not so necessary as the prodigious extension of the railway establishment has perhaps rendered it. The few who can recall the time of which I write will warmly acknowledge the truth of these remarks.

CHAPTER VI.

UNDER the new organisation the line was divided into districts. In the locomotive department we had Mr. Edward Bury for the south, Mr. Ramsbottom and Mr. Trevithic for the north. In the coaching department Mr. H. P. Bruyeres for the south, Mr. Norris, superintendent and engineer, for the north. The goods department was managed by Mr. Mills in the south, Mr. Eborall, central district, at Birmingham, Mr. Poole at Liverpool, and Mr. Salt at Manchester. Mr. Eborall was the father of Mr. Cornelius Eborall, who became for many years the esteemed General Manager of the South Eastern Railway, and whose death, at a comparatively early age, was deeply lamented.

In 1847 it was decided to abolish the system of toll carrying, and the Railway Company gradually commenced carrying directly for the public. Pickford & Co. and Chaplin and Horne being appointed agents for the cartage of the traffic, and to work the Goods sheds in London.

1847.

A monthly Conference of the Goods Managers and the Agents, presided over by Captain Huish, was instituted, at which the bitter quarrels of Pickford & Co. and Chaplin and Horne were the most remarkable feature. Their implacable competition with one another, in seeking the trade, was a source of weakness to the Company; for the agents would expend as much strength in getting customers from one another as in drawing them from railways and other competitive services. Pickford & Co. withdrew their boats from the canals, and Chaplin and Horne, who were almost new to the goods traffic, matured their position by means of their old Coaching connection and parcels offices. Mr. Horne threw all his excitable and inexhaustible energy into the combat; while the three sons of Mr. Baxendale took the management of Pickford & Co.'s department with increased personal feeling and angry opposition.

The North London Line to Fenchurch Street and Poplar was opened in 1846, and at the suggestion of Mr. Horne the London and North Western Company purchased some Dock Warehouses at Haydon Square, Aldgate, and formed a Goods Station for the City at that place. I accompanied the first goods train to Haydon, about four o'clock one fine summer morning, and the view of all the sleeping uncurtained rooms of the squalid houses which the train commanded was, indeed, only "a sight for a father." The North London Company added to my other duties, by consent of the London and North Western Company, the office of goods manager, at a small, but to me important, salary; at that time Mr. Harry Chubb was the secretary. He was an able manager, a just and considerate master, an amiable and refined gentleman, and a sincere friend.

The work of uniting all the railways in the Clearing House, for the division of the receipts, the making of rates, and a system of accounts for a universal carrying, with all the consequent details, was a great labour, but it progressed quickly in the hands of the able goods managers and accountants to whom it was entrusted, and the new arrangement approached completion. Periodical conferences of the officers of all the railways in the Clearing House were established, and a code of rules for the business was printed. Had the Companies at the same time taken in hand the management of the cartage, within a radius of their respective stations, they would very easily have transferred to themselves all the men who actually did the work, and by rejecting the large firms who absorbed so much of the profit (and who should have disappeared with the coaches, or confined themselves to the canals and suburb carrying), would have saved enormous cost and many years of dispute and difficulty, yet unsettled; while the public would have been drawn nearer to them, and the question of a reduction in rates would have pressed less heavily. Cartage at a cost price leaves the railway rate to be discussed on its merits. Cartage by a contractor, who requires a large profit, exhausts the elasticity of the railway rate. Without the cartage in their own hands, therefore, this beautiful system of carrying, which conferred such a great benefit on the trade of the country, was crippled and incomplete. The public require the movement of their merchandise to be one transaction from the door to the destination, and any intermediate dealer is an extra cost and obstruction. Better far would it have been for the peace of the Companies to have continued their carrying on toll, and left the public to the irregular and uncontrolled charges of town carriers, great and small.

It may be urged that competition between the carters would have reduced the charges to the minimum; but even in the Canal time these carriers learned how to combine to keep up prices, and they are still, as then, uncontrolled by Acts of Parliament, by Railway Commissioners, or even by public opinion. I may also state that the charges for the porterage (that is, the delivery) of packages conveyed by coach, in the old Road time, were oppressively exorbitant, and altogether irregular and unchecked.

Much more could be said on this subject, but it is controversial ground, and I desire only to write a sketch of the experience of a very humble member of the Railway body during a period somewhat interesting, and that only within the limits of my own immediate sphere.

Amongst the changes related I had obtained some promotion, being appointed chief assistant to Mr. Mills, who was now much engaged with other managers in the formation of the altered arrangements. I had also the charge of the Camden Station, trains, brakesmen, etc., with partial responsibility to Mr. Bruyeres, the superintendent of the southern division. My salary was advanced, which enabled me to take a wife; an event having much more to do with the good working of a railway officer than is sometimes supposed.

During this period of steady duty, there were some "cakes and ale." The first Officers' Dinner took place at the Euston Hotel, then newly built. Mr. Kenneth Morison presided, and I wrote, and sang, a song, which was graciously received. We had a cricket club on the fields now covered by the Gloucester Road at Camden. Among the members were Mr. Samuel

Brooks and Mr. Dawson, who whistled duets in sweet fashion; amiable George Coulter, a hard hitter at cricket, who gave me one to long-field which I caught on my eye; the two Chapmans; the two Bacons, of the Hotel; Thomas Long; J. O. Binger; and many others; of whom I alone remain in the service—and even my cricketing days are long gone by. Groups of faces of the young and merry companions of the Stores office, the Goods office, the Booking and Audit offices at Euston, etc., rise up to my memory. William Haley, a happy bachelor, with a sweet voice and exquisite taste; poor Stephen Beadle; bluff Tom Holbein; Jacob the messenger, droll as Sam Weller; pompous but good-hearted Bickley; handsome Tom Barker—la-di-da—who once thought he gave me a great treat by taking me to see Tom Cribb the bruiser, who appeared to me anything but a representative of muscular beauty; Brennan; Sadgrove; Tyers; James Hewett; Henry Whittle; Penrucker; Oliver; and others: all talented, musical, or in some way amusing—lightening the long hours by many a joke; all long since gone, by death and change, in foreign lands or otherwise, and succeeded by repeated relays of others, as the decades have proceeded.

I found time in the early Camden Goods years to attend lectures, learn mechanics, and study design at Somerset House, under Mr. Dyce, R.A., and music under Mr. Hullah; and I had occasional treats at the theatre in Macready's days, with a chop afterwards at Paddy Green's entertainment at Evan's Grand Hotel, where I took down the songs in shorthand, for my friend William Haley. The money-taker at this establishment had a curious method of making fourteen-pence one and fourpence, and sixteen-pence one and sixpence, greatly to his profit. He had a large hole in his forehead, which, perhaps, caused the mathematical peculiarity.

In my early youth, I had become familiar with the forms of most of the aristocratic celebrities, by visits to the park, etc.; Count D'Orsay, with his magnificent whiskers, his splendid cabriolet drawn by two horses, with a bright steel bar across them; the old Duke of Wellington; the Fitz Clarences; Sir Watkin Wynne, on his stout cob; Lord Melbourne; Lord Forester; Lord Chesterfield, etc., so that when any of them came to the Railway, which at first was considered a subject of curiosity rather than an established institution, I could point them out. I have seen the great Sir Robert Peel draw down a white night-cap over his wise head, as he settled himself in a carriage for a night journey by rail; Lord Brougham borrow paper and postage-stamps from the booking clerk; and I had the honour to help Mr. P. Hardwick, the company's architect, to exhibit to Queen Adelaide the then new machine for catching the mail bags on the railway journey. Daniel O'Connel frequently used the line, and wore a blue cloth cap, which made him look like a large sized master of a German band.

I also recognised the members of the theatrical profession; for, when a boy, a friend, who had dealings with the theatres, gave me opportunities of carrying business communications to them, and in my visits to Mr. Palmer, of Drury Lane, I often lingered on the bridge above the stage to listen to the singing of Madame Malibran, or the declamation of Macready, Helen Fawcet, and many others. I was in the Strand theatre one morning and heard W. J. Hammond give Douglas Jerrold an account of a violent personal encounter on the previous day, between Alfred Bunn—"velvet breeches Bunn"—and Macready. The quarrel, which might have resulted in murder, was through some jealousy of Macready's as to Charles Kean. On another occasion, at Covent Garden, I was swept away from the slips by a ballet retreating to clear the front. I had once an opportunity to call on Harley, the great comedian, in Gower Street, but was so overcome by the comicality of his approach to me, that I had a great difficulty to tell my business for laughter.

On another occasion, I had to see Macready in his dressing-room, at the Haymarket. He was studying his part. At the conclusion of my message he turned tragically to me, and bit out his thanks, adding that he would send me an order for the gallery. Much hurt, and indignant, I bowed and retired. I had rare chances of seeing that beautiful woman, and talented actress and songstress, Madame Vestris. At the conclusion of a conversation with Mr. Palmer, she once said, "Ah! Mr. Palmer, some day you will see me a faded figure at the corner of a street, begging, and people will say, 'That is the celebrated Madame Vestris!'"

Palmer never had that grief, although she was extravagant to the last. While touching on theatrical experiences, I may relate that in later years, at some private performances at the house of a friend, I met a modest young gentleman who was then, I think, engaged in the wine trade. He played "Boots at the Swan" admirably, and recited some pieces of his own composition, and in after conversation was strongly recommended by me and others to adopt the stage as a profession. He afterwards did so, and with what success the name of J. L. Toole is sufficient to tell.

The lawyers too were known to me. In my holidays, when quite a boy, I had a habit of attending the Law Courts, to listen to the trials. Ballantine and Parry, who were then leaders at the Old Bailey, always on opposite sides, were at once recognised when they appeared. Many a pleasant time have I passed in laughing at the witty pleadings and clever cross-examination of Charles Phillips, afterwards Commissioner in Bankruptcy, and the sad victim of a misunderstanding on the trial of Courvoisier, for the murder of Lord William Russell. I happened to be in court at the trial of a Chartist, whom the Attorney General Jarvis prosecuted and Kenealy defended, when the latter was rebuked for his strong language to Mr. Attorney. He used stronger language on the Tichborne trial years afterwards. I was present at part of the trial of Hocker, for the murder of his friend Delarue. Both had been teachers of languages at Hampstead, and Hocker had been a constant attendant at the Parish Church. He at one time sought to pay his addresses to the daughter of a widow lady of my acquaintance, and she commissioned me to see him and make inquiries as to his respectability. I met Hocker and found him to be an educated but flighty and conceited young man. For this and other reasons I reported against his eligibility. A year, probably, afterwards, returning home to Hampstead one night, I was told that a man had been killed in a field next the wall of the extensive grounds surrounding Belsize House, now covered by the houses called Belsize Gardens. The murderer, as it afterwards appeared, left his victim and ran across the field to the Swiss Cottage, washing his hands in the snow on the way; and, after fortifying himself with some brandy, returned to the spot and assisted to carry the body to the Yorkshire Grey at

Hampstead. Hocker was afterwards cleverly traced to be the murderer, and offered, as his defence, the unlikely story that he had accompanied the brother of a young lady at Hampstead, to chastise Delarue for misconduct towards her. The brother, he averred, struck the fatal blow, but he, Hocker, being engaged to the young lady, could not betray the brother, or he would be a traitor. If he suffered for the offence, he would die a martyr. This defence, the police told me, the counsel rejected as entirely against the evidence; but the authorities thought it necessary to make an inquiry at Hampstead, to discover any love affair that might have existed, and somehow found the little matter of my friend the widow lady's daughter, and my inquiry. In consequence of which the police called at my lodgings and searched the lady's house, in a very rough and painful way, confiscating some of Hocker's letters which they discovered, as great prizes of detection. The circumstance caused endless excitement and reports, and a long period of serious annoyances, but the Sheriff afterwards obtained, in writing, from the prisoner, a complete statement that he had not the slightest intention to allude in the most remote degree to my young friend.

Captain Moorsom became Admiral Moorsom, and Chairman of the Chester and Holyhead Railway; J. O. Binger General Manager of that Railway, and Robert Mansell, brother of Dean Mansell, the Secretary. The line was afterwards amalgamated with the London and North Western, when Mr. Binger was appointed superintendent of the Chester and Holyhead district, and, Mr. Chubb having retired, Mr. Mansell came to the North London Line, which was always mainly the property of the London and North Western Company. The Admiral succeeded to the chair of the London and North Western Board in 1861, after the retirement of the Marquis of Chandos. Mr. Glyn had retired in 1853, and had been succeeded first by General Anson and then by the Marquis of Chandos. This nobleman had made his name heroic by cutting off the entail of his father's estate, to pay the Duke's creditors, and had to devote his energies to work, to sustain the consequences. Previous to his appointment he was inspecting the departments of the railway and called at Mr. Bruyeres' office. Poor Watts, a clerk, who was somewhat impressed with his own official dignity, asked his lordship what he wanted —" a situation? If so, there are no vacancies. Besides, you're too short." The Marquis replied, "Then I will leave my card" "Oh, your card. Very well." But when Watts read the card he fell down and worshipped, and never smiled again.

Old Mr. Creed, the Secretary, retired in September, 1848, and was succeeded by Mr. C. E. Stewart.

Mr. Stewart had seen foreign service in the civil department of Government, and was a gentleman eminently qualified for his new position. During my communication with him he received an anonymous letter charging me with purloining the Company's property. He sent for me and bade me read it, and then asked if I knew how he intended to dispose of it—immediately putting it into the fire. Captain Huish entered at the moment, and, on being told the circumstances, requested me if I could find the author, to take legal proceedings, and the Company would bear the expense. He said it would doubtless be found to have been sent by some discharged man : which turned out to be the case.

The Secretary's duty at this time was less classified from the General Manager's than after Mr. Cawkwell's period, and Mr. Stewart received applications for railway evidence in parliament and elsewhere. He did me the honour to nominate me as L. & N. W. witness in a great number of cases—service which was often very remunerative and much missed by me in after days, having given evidence in every court of judicature, from the House of Lords to the Coroner's Inquest. In later years Mr. Stewart nominated me for the post of Agent to the Great Indian Peninsular Railway, in Bombay, at £3,000 per annum, which I should have obtained but for Captain Sherrard Osborne, who brought greater interest in his favour at the last moment.

Mr. Edward Bury's four-wheeled engines had been the subject of much controversy in the railway newspapers. They were superior to any previously used, but were not strong enough for the traffic; he retired in March, '47. He had been of great service to the Company, not only in his own department. He was succeeded by Mr. McConnell, a strong and determined man of the rough sort. By the aid of Mr. Madigan of the

Permanent Way Department, and others, he successfully resisted a strike of the engine-drivers. The guards who rode on the engine-plate, to direct the new men, received printed certificates of special service during this serious difficulty.

Mr. McConnell's "Bloomers," 7-6 fly-wheel, and six-wheeled coupled engines, were a great success and made his name. He was the author of many locomotive improvements and patents, which brought him wealth, and he afterwards retired to Aylesbury, became a member of the County Bench of magistrates, and sat, in that capacity, with Disraeli. I received many acts of hospitable courtesy at his hands, as well as offers of appointments on foreign railways.

In Mr. Stewart's Secretaryship before Captain Huish retired, Mr. Edward Watkin became an under Secretary. He took an active part in all the important transactions of the Company, and exhibited talent of no ordinary kind. Had he remained he would doubtless have succeeded to the highest position, but he sought "pastures new," and is now Sir Edward Watkin, Bart. Under his direction I was commissioned to contest the re-election of some of the members of the Parochial Board of the St. Pancras Parish—that body having behaved in an arbitrary manner to the Company. We were defeated in the first contest, but when the new Metropolitan Management Act came into force, a new Board of respectable and in many cases distinguished men were elected and took their seats under the chairmanship of the Rev. Thomas Dale, Vicar of the Parish. I represented the Company, and added to my experience as Chairman of the Assessment Rate and Appeal Committee.

While the years were gliding by and the everlasting principles of change and renewal were operating on the railway, as in all things, the traffic increased, and branch lines and amalgamations were added to the L. & N. W. Company. The stations and appliances became too small—were always, in fact, behind the requirements, and officers and servants were too frequently condemned and removed, instead of the real remedy of suitable enlargement being promptly applied. The coal grew, from small beginnings, into a heavy traffic. When the Clay Cross Company first proposed to send coals by rail to London, it is said that Mr. Bruyeres would not receive it from the Midland Company, at Rugby, unless it were restricted to a few wagon loads at a time, covered carefully with tarpaulins—a restriction that speedily gave way. The first consignment of Clay Cross coal by rail to London was brought to Kilburn Station in July 1845, and was sold by Mr. Baker, a gentleman still in the employment of the Clay Cross Company. The Ince Hall Coal was shortly afterwards sent by Messrs. Lee and Jerdein. The cattle traffic necessitated the erection of a large cattle station at Camden. The animals, who always, in their excitement, ran the wrong way, often escaped on to the main line and charged the trains, getting, of course, the worst of such encounters. The cattle landing was ultimately removed to the Maiden Lane Station, which reduced, but never entirely stopped, such casualties. These were not confined to bullocks from the cattle pens. A sharp watchman, in a dimly lighted goods shed at Camden, once found a bear, which had escaped from Euston, crouching against a waggon, and, taking it for a thief, he pounced upon it, but retreated in dismay, unhurt. A hue-and-cry was raised, and poor Bruin was captured, after a spirited chase. At another time a tiger in a case fell from a load on to the railway. The fall smashed the case, and the tiger trotted along the line. Some soldiers were obtained from a neighbouring barrack and went in pursuit. They found that the signalman had climbed a telegraph post to get out of the way, but on nearing the tiger they discovered that they had marched without ammunition, and the tiger fell to the gun of a gentleman who lived near the spot. A case containing a crocodile similarly fell from a train, and an inspector, walking the line, thought he was nearing a man run over, but he speedily went back for assistance, on arriving at the object of his attention.

CHAPTER VII.

IN August, 1846, Mr. Glyn cautioned the proprietors as to the probable decrease in the value of the property, and in February, 1847, a reduction of the dividend was declared for the last half of 1846. Dissatisfaction ensued, which continued until 1851, when Mr. Richard Moon was elected a Director. This gentleman immediately took a very active part in the affairs of the Company, and was appointed, with two other Directors, to examine the whole working of the establishment. The departments were at this time imperfectly controlled by head quarters. Different systems prevailed in the Districts, according to the differing views of the Managers and Superintendents. The Goods Managers made their own rates. The purchase of stores was extravagantly conducted, and the sale of old materials was open to irregularities and dishonesty. The check departments were insufficient, and the discipline of the staff was loose; while passes for free travelling were issued by all departments and were shamefully abused. Matters which appeared insignificant, compared with the principal transactions of the Company, yet involving the expenditure of large sums of money, were left entirely in the hands of officers in receipt of small salaries: and some of them proved unworthy of their trust. In short, the then unusually large establishment appeared incapable of effective management by ordinary methods. Yet Mr. Moon brought to the task he and his colleagues had undertaken the simple maxims of an industrious and vigilant merchant. By expanding them to the magnitude of the concern, he believed that he could make it thoroughly well governed and completely disciplined. He ultimately succeeded, after many years of untiring labour, amidst opposition of every kind; and the voluminous programme of reforms which he registered during the searching investigation he had made was finally completed by the removal of the Agents from the possession of the London Goods Stations, ten years afterwards.

De mortuis nil nsi bonum is not the rule of the historian. It is of the dead he speaks freely; of the living he is silent. I ask for an exception in the case of Mr. Moon, in describing him as a man of grave aspect, with a pleasant smile, enhanced by its rarity; always approachable to those of his officers in whom he believed. He had a single eye for the Company's interest, an insatiable capacity for details, and a belief in a personal examination of every person and place on whom or which a decision was necessary. After he became Chairman, his unadorned addresses to the proprietors were like familiar conversations between the head of a firm and his partners. Such a reformer was inevitably unpopular. Many of the Directors, and more of the officers, from the Manager downwards, decried his recommendations and opposed him. He was condemned as mean, self-seeking, and petty in his views—partial in his appointment of officers—and ungrateful for earnest services—unjust to old servants, and capricious and conceited of his own views. I believe I was the first man who worked heartily with him, and, so far as could be consistent with the difference of our rank, a mutual friendship was soon established between us. For many years, no week passed without our exchanging written communications. Mr. Moon was alike indifferent to good or evil repute and tenaciously pursued the even tenor of his way, until, as I have said, he carried all his points in time. Change in the Directorate, and the manifestly good results of his measures, brought him supporters. The Marquis of Chandos retired, and Admiral Moorsom succeeded to the Chairmanship. In 1861 the latter died, and Mr. Moon was appointed to the office. From this date commenced that steady course of improvement and enlightened progress which has enabled the Railway to take its place as one of the most complete organisations in the world, and the leading line of this kingdom. The perfect supervision of every department of the establishment by Committees of Directors, the careful choice of managers and staff, the soundness of the plant the enterprising and wise expenditure to widen and extend the line to meet the increasing traffic, the constant additions to the comforts and safety of travelling—are all unsurpassed, if in any way equalled, in this or any other country; while not the least is to be commended the liberal treatment of the officers and staff in providing for their retirement and old age. Before this consummation could be approached, Mr. Moon had many years of active service and constant labour, many disappointments, and much to call forth and exercise his indomitable courage and persistence.

In the Stores Department Mr. Chapman was removed, and the system of purchase entirely altered. In the Goods Mr. Eborall died and was replaced by Mr. Broughton. Mr Braithwaite Poole, of Liverpool, and Mr. Salt, of Manchester, left the service. Mr. Poole had been made the first Chief Goods Manager by Captain Huish. He was an accomplished and clever man, and a delightful social companion. He wrote some useful compilations for railway work, and was highly appreciated at the Railway Clearing House Committees; but he was far too ambitious, and too indifferent to the details of his department, to suit the ideas of the Chairman. Some blot was discovered in Mr. Salt's management, in which his assistant, Mr. Kay, was involved, but the latter speedily regained the confidence of his superiors. He was appointed temporarily to manage part of the goods of the Manchester District, and Mr. Noden was put over another part. Mr. Mills was removed to Euston and succeeded Mr. Poole as Chief Goods Manager. I succeeded to his district; Mr. Huntley to Wolverhampton. We were thus a new Goods Conference, under the chairmanship of Mr. Mills; Mr. Broughton acting as Secretary. A General Conference of all the officers, Superintendents of the Coaching Department and Goods Managers, was also formed, under the chairmanship of the General Manager.

As time sped, and Mr. Moon had almost completed his programme of reforms, the last item, namely, the removal of the Agents from the shed work of the London stations, came to the front. Captain Huish had resigned, and Mr. Cawkwell, from the Lancashire and Yorkshire Railway, was appointed General Manager; but he and some of the Directors did not sympathise with this important change. Mr. Charles Mason, who had joined the Company as chief Goods Manager on the superannuation of Mr. Mills, had scarcely yet grasped his department. Messrs. Pickford and Co., and Messrs. Chaplin and Horne were, of course, bitterly opposed to their removal from the stations, and they had many staunch friends at the Board. Much discussion ensued, but the Chairman persevered; and, finally, I consummated my many reports on the subject by a statement at the Board. I was exposed to a severe cross-examination for some hours, resulting in a favourable vote and many unexpected compliments on the manner in which I had sustained the ordeal. Mr. Horne, who had implied that he should abide by the decision of the Directors, and either hoped for a different result or thought Pickford and Co. would resist, became furious. He applied for an injunction, and the case was tried, Sir Hugh Cairns advocating the Company's case. The injunction was refused, and from that time Mr. Horne pursued me with unrelenting persecution. He left nothing undone, no vituperation unsaid, to ruin me with the Directors and the management.

The Goods establishment in London was transferred to the Company, giving me nights and days of labour and anxiety; the Chairman alone in any way helping me with advice, assistance or authority.

The general organisation was soon brought into form, although Pickford & Co. carried away nearly all the best men. I had to find an accountant from the staff of Chaplin and Horne. He succumbed to the numberless obstructions of the agents, who had ample means of active annoyance in the cartage accounts. The invoice tissue copies were often mysteriously destroyed or missing, and it became evident that a stronger man should take the work in hand. Mr. Ephraim Wood, from the Audit Office, at Euston, was chosen, and, after many months of skilful industry and determination, brought the accounts to a balance, and triumphantly placed this part of the work in perfect order. He received deserved promotions for his exertions.

In looking for a chief assistant I displeased Mr. Reay, who was then the chief of the Audit Office, by endeavouring to obtain Mr. Houghton for the appointment. He was willing to come, but Mr. Reay valued his assistance, and I at length accepted Mr. Stewart's nominee, Mr. Briscoe, who had been a soldier in the celebrated charge of the Light Brigade at Balaclava. He was an able and active man, and was soon removed to a more important post.

After the removal of the agents, a few years of tolerably regular work ensued, always accompanied by Mr. Horne's never ceasing attacks.

CHAPTER VIII.

PRIOR to these events, as previously stated, Mr. Mills was placed on the retired list. I had the best authority for hoping that I should succeed him, but the completion of the work at Camden tied me to that place, and I lost the chance. Mr. Reay, of the Audit Office, was proposed, but Mr. Charles Mason, who had competed for the general managership, was ultimately chosen. He came from the Birkenhead Railway, and was a shrewd and indefatigable man of business, after the Chairman's own heart; a disciplinarian, but ever considerate to those under him; sharp and decided with real offenders, but reluctant to find fault, and desirous of being friendly and cheery with his subordinates, which gave force to deserved rebukes.

The business grew, until it was evident that the goods stations in London were too small for the traffic. Space was purchased near Broad Street for a large City Station. While Broad Street Station was preparing, a proposition arose for the erection of a large shed at Camden, in which to treat the goods on an altered principle—a system which no one who knows the details of the London work would approve. I could not succeed in convincing the Directors and the Management that the plan would certainly fail. I intimated that the scheme should wait until Broad Street Depôt became completed, and the effect upon Camden should be ascertained. I was told that Broad Street would take little of the traffic from Camden. The opening of the City Station proved the correctness of my representations.

Whether it was considered that I should not give the new method fair play, or that Mr. Horne's incessant reports and violent tirades became intolerable, I do not know; but it was decided that a gentleman from Manchester, who was said to understand the proposed mode of working, should carry out the change. I had visited Manchester with Mr. Mason, but could find no system in operation with miscellaneous goods such as those in London. When the shed was finished Mr. Greenish was appointed, and I was removed to Euston, and was appointed to take charge of an enlarged southern district of the Goods Department, extending from Kensington to near Stafford and Birmingham, including the branch lines intervening, and after a short period, with the further charge of opening the Company's new stations at Leicester and Derby, and the new development of the Midland Collieries, and the Ashby-de-la-Zouch Railway, with the outlying agencies at Leicester, Newark, Gloucester, Cheltenham, Worcester and Southampton.

Meanwhile the new system was commenced, and, as I had predicted, it threw the provincial work into such confusion, that in a few days its failure had to be admitted and the old method resumed.

My office at Euston being considered insufficiently central for my new work, Mr. Cawkwell informed me that I should remove to Rugby. To leave London was a severe trial to me. I left my friends and the pleasant associations of many years. I ceased to be a member of the Clearing House Goods Conference, and lost much of my position with Mr. Mason, whom, as I have said, I had assisted to manage the line during Mr. Cawkwell's continued absence.

During the absence of Mr. Cawkwell through ill health Mr. Mason considered it necessary to give me assistance, in order that I might aid him in negotiations with other Companies, increased duties, parliamentary and others, at Euston, and as no eligible person on the line appeared available, I was instructed to find a suitable Railway man elsewhere. I at first selected Mr. John Noble of the Clearing House. The terms I offered were considered insufficient by Mr. Noble. He afterwards took service with the Midland Company, and ultimately became the General Manager of that line. I next appointed Mr. Lambert of the Great Eastern. He closed with my proposals, and assisted me as previously recorded, first in the district at Northampton and afterwards in charge of the London Stations. On Mr. Cawkwell's return sometime afterwards, the arrangement for my removal to Rugby and Mr. Greenish to Camden, no provision for Mr. Lambert appeared to have been considered, and, on enquiry as to what duties he was to fulfil under the change, he was ordered to take a subordinate appointment under Mr. Greenish, which, considering that the country portion of the division was to be taken away with me, was a fall to Mr. Lambert. He seemed to think he had been brought away from the Great Eastern under a misrepresentation, and, as I felt personally concerned in the good faith towards him, I introduced him to Mr. Grant, the General Goods Manager of the Great Western, who, on my representation of his high qualities, immediately engaged him. The change was fortunate for Mr. Lambert, who subsequently succeeded Mr. Grant, on that gentleman's lamented death, and in later times obtained the position of General Manager of the Great Western Railway. Mr. Grant was profuse in his thanks to me on several occasions as to the benefit I brought to his Company by the transfer of Mr. Lambert.

I had now to resign my commission as Captain in the Middlesex Artillery Volunteers, of which corps the Duke of Buckingham was Colonel. My weekly attendance at the Coal Exchange was to continue, and was a little relief to my exile. Occasional kindness from Mr. Mason and the chairman also consoled me. The circumstances of the case rendered them powerless to prevent my removal, but did not lose me their confidence. I started to take possession of my duties at Rugby one Sunday night, but on reaching Euston I was so heart-sick and unhappy that I returned to my home in town and went the next morning. The new work and the fresh air of the country soon restored my spirits, and I settled down in the position as a permanent thing for the rest of my service. Advance in salary and frequent recognition of work conscientiously done helped me to forget disappointments, and, as I considered, my unjust treatment.

Additions in these years were made to the Goods Conference. Mr. D. Parsons, Mr. Carter, Mr. Bradshaw, and occasionally Mr. George Findlay, from South Wales, became members; Mr. Mason, and, in his absence, myself, presiding. In time the Company purchased the South Wales line, and, with it, Mr. Findlay was transferred to the London and North Western service. Ultimately he came to London and was made General Goods Manager, Mr. Mason taking the post of Assistant General

Manager. Mr. Horne found his match in Mr. Findlay. The former had been in the habit of visiting Euston, carrying in his hands his hat, and in his pockets a confusion of papers. He would call at one office and exclaim

"Ah, Manager No. 1 Out;
Gone fishing, no doubt!"

—at another and say,

"Of course, Manager No. 2
Gone fishing also!"

—at another and say,

"Manager Mason gone to look after
His cracked stones!"

But he had occasion to abandon that kind of conduct with Mr. Findlay, who subdued him very considerably in a little time; although he never ceased to rage, and Mr. Greenish fared as badly with him a I had done. When very ill Mr. Horne rose from his sick-bed and came to the conference, and Mr. Findlay addressed to him some congratulatory words as to his returning health. He replied with angry remarks, condemning all the officers wholesale. Soon afterwards his restless and wearied spirit found the common fate of us all, and his place knew him no more. He did good service during his fretful hour on the stage of life, and his eccentricities, on the whole, provoked more smiles than anger.

About this time Mr. Robert Savill, the Assistant Secretary, was superannuated. He had been with the London and Birmingham portion of the line from the formation of the Company, and was universally esteemed by the staff and the public. In this year of the Queen's Jubilee [1887] he is still alive and vigorous, and continues his useful life in the sphere in which he moves, as a private gentleman.

Mr. Reay, of the Audit Office, became Secretary, *vice* Mr. Stewart, who retired and soon after died. Mr. Coldwell succeeded Mr. Reay in the Audit Department, and died after a comparatively short enjoyment of his position; Mr. Partington succeeding him.

In the past decade there had been still occasional "Cakes and Ale." In the Marquis of Chandos's reign he invited a number of Directors and Officers, and their wives, to a fête at his country residence, and we enjoyed boating and feasting and the hospitable society of the Marquis and Marchioness. On another occasion I accompanied my volunteer regiment to the Battle of Stowe. We were quartered with the Yeomanry Cavalry. My Company was told off to the fortress in the grounds, and I am afraid that if our guns had been shotted we should have slain many of our friends. The Monthly Conference always dined together and enjoyed many hours of pleasant intercourse. Of such meetings Mr. Dudley Parsons was the leading spirit. At the Officers' meetings, during Captain Huish's time at Birmingham, we had always a formal meal after the work. At one of these gatherings we bade farewell to Mr. Slater, of the Carriage Department, who resigned, on which occasion I wrote an impromptu song, and had the assurance to sing it. At another of these meetings Mr. Cawkwell changed chairs with Captain Huish, on the latter's retirement. Then, the retirement of any of the Managers was always celebrated by a testimonial, present and a dinner; Dudley Parsons, the provider and king of the feast. The vacancies by death and change had been replaced by Mr. David Taylor at Liverpool, Mr. Farr at Manchester, Mr. John Mason at Birmingham, and others. Districts were altered and extended, and other members were added to the conference. The monthly social meetings were merged into an annual dinner, which came off at some place away from town—the Crystal Palace, Richmond, Malvern, Windermere, &c., under my secretaryship, after Mr. Parsons left the service. All these occasions were pleasant breaks in our official toil.

The sudden death of Mr. Charles Mason was a shock to us all, and extinguished in me any remaining hope of further promotion in the service. Besides which, in him I lost a true and real personal friend. Many a happy evening I can recall, spent with him in star-watching, with his powerful telescope, or with the Royal Astronomical Society, of which he was a fellow; many a day's shooting in the holidays, and many hours of pleasant work in deciding knotty questions relating to the business of the line, or in drawing up reports. After Mr. Mason's death, Mr. George Findlay was appointed Assistant General Manager, and I began to revive a little hope that the office of Chief Goods Manager might fall to me. It became apparent, however, that Mr. Thomas

Kay was nominated. While the matter was under discussion, Mr. Kay generously proposed to me to ask the Directors to divide the appointment into two, North and South. The proposal was made, but rejected, and Mr. Kay succeeded to the appointment; for a time he remained at Manchester, but afterwards came to London.

Without any feeling of envy for Mr. Kay, whose worthy and honest character I greatly admired, I felt the disappointment keenly. It was no reflection on me to be displaced by such a man as Mr. Mason or Mr. Findlay, but, as compared with Mr. Kay, I was the older servant and slightly the senior manager. I had greater experience, both in the management of a large establishment and in the highest management of the concern, and was better acquainted with the general affairs of the Company. I may add, without egotism, that I was better educated. The Duke of Buckingham, from whom I had always received the most kindly recognition, meeting me at this time, offered me some consoling remarks, saying he supposed it was "a descent of the Normans." Some pleasant words from the Chairman and a little time, with the reflection that the Directors had a right to set up or put down whomsoever they pleased, brought me back to my usual cheerful condition of mind, and I gave to Mr. Kay, my cordial and loyal co-operation, "as in duty bound." He was afterwards assisted by the appointment of Mr. Houghton to the post of Assistant Goods Manager.

My residence in Warwickshire obtained for me many new friends, among them Mr. Newdegate, M.P., to whom I rendered a little service in regard to his estate. He placed me on the free list of his newspaper, and never ceased to treat me with marked consideration until his death. My few leisure hours were spent in the delights of my large garden, or in advocating in the local press some contested improvements in the affairs of the place, under a *nom de plume* which became well known. The beauty of the country through which I travelled in my daily rounds, at all seasons gave me intense enjoyment, and made me conscious that there was something to see in the world besides the rough and tumble excitement of railway work. I found amusement in the characters of traders with whom I had to deal, and food or observation in the social cliques and parties of the towns where I transacted business. I began to think myself too old for any further notice by my railway superiors. I thought my little career had culminated, and was content and happy during some very pleasant years.

CHAPTER IX.

IN the early part of the year 1877, I was privately informed that the original design of taking over the Agency of Messrs. Chaplin and Horne was to be consummated. When the idea was first entertained, during Mr. Charles Mason's Goods Managership, and when my difficulties with Mr. Horne were in full force, I had been named for the future management of this work. I now thought I might still be considered qualified for the post. The hope gave me new life. In the end, I received the appointment, and came to London to commence one of the most arduous undertakings that had hitherto fallen to my lot. I found the town offices in a very confused and irregular condition, as regards charges, check, and discipline. The cartage irregularly and expensively worked, and the canvassing department unsystematic. Five or six years of incessant labour and attention absorbed the offices into the railway method of audit and supervision. The cartage and canvassing were organised into districts. New premises in several parts of London were opened, and the old offices improved. The Agency was altogether made to cover the Metropolis with useful means of communication by the public with the Company's main establishment, and advertised the London and North Western Railway more prominently than it had ever been préviously. The arrangements in degree contributed to the great popularity which has lately marked the progress of the railway, and helped to establish it as the acknowledged leader of the British railways. I attribute the success of these efforts mainly to the freedom of action kindly accorded to me during the early years of the change. I had not the usual, and, as a rule, necessary interference with the proceedings. I carried out my views, and reported the results to the General Manager and the Committee, formed for the purpose, under the Chairman of the Company. I understood the business, and enjoyed the confidence of my superiors; and it was a labor of love in the city I understood best, and which was the place in all the world I most valued. My banishment had been indeed to me an exile, and I may be pardoned a little feeling of triumph at returning to the scene of my severe persecution in a position of trust and command. Ten years have rapidly past, and in the course of that time the Agency has become welded into the Company's establishment, and duly subjected to the departments and regulations of the railway. The saving in the expenses paid off the purchase money in the first three years, and the progress has been satisfactorily continued up to the present time; notwithstanding many circumstances adverse to the parcels trade. The whole of the London Stations, during recent years, have been added to my charge, in all composing a staff of nearly three thousand hands, and many hundreds of horses.

The London places for the reception of goods and parcels and for other conveniences of the public are as follows, viz. :—

NUMBER OF GOODS STATIONS, OFFICES, &c.

	No.
Goods Stations	5
Outlying Stations, Goods and Coal	22
Coal Depôts only	3
Town Offices	33
London and North Western Stations, Parcel Offices	10
Do. Universal Offices, Goods and Parcels	5
North London Stations, Parcels Offices	18
Do. Universal Offices, Goods and Parcels	8
West London Stations, Parcels Offices	4
	108
Pickford and Companys' Goods and Parcels Offices	25
Auxiliary do.	15
	40
Total	148

I am now fulfilling the final years of my service, and while I apologise for this somewhat self laudatory record of to me the most enjoyable part of my career, I venture to hope for a belief in the minds of my employers that I have executed my trust.

While I have been occupied with trade and shipping—customs and bills of lading—warehouses—barges—carts and horses—sales—markets—exhibitions and theatrical parties and ships crews, and so dealing with all sorts and conditions of men in this vast Metropolis, what of the line? Many writers have told the tale of its wondrous advancement. Science has been busy with the Engines, the Signals, and the Brakes, taste and comfort in the Carriage have occupied the best efforts of the Mechanic and Upholsterer—and the perfection in travelling has culminated in the Royal and other trains. Long may the goodly work continue, and the prosperity of the dear old country render it necessary when my humble pen shall have lost its cunning, and my little share of duty as one of the pioneers of the great invention shall be forgotten in the dust.

London & Birmingham
RAILWAY.

HOURS OF DEPARTURE.
COMMENCING 29th OCTOBER, 1837.

From London:
FIRST TRAIN	- - -	8 o'Clock A.M.
SECOND do.	- -	10 o'Clock A.M.
THIRD do.	- -	2 o'Clock P.M.
FOURTH do.	- -	5 o'Clock P.M.

From Tring:
FIRST TRAIN	- - -	8 o'Clock A.M.
SECOND do.	- -	10 o'Clock A.M.
THIRD do.	- -	2 o'Clock P.M.
FOURTH do.	- -	7 o'Clock P.M.

Every Monday Morning, the First Train from Tring will leave at Seven, instead of Eight.

ON SUNDAYS,
FROM
London and Tring:
FIRST TRAIN	-	½ past 9 o'Clock A.M.
SECOND do.	-	½ past 1 o'Clock P.M.
THIRD do.	- -	5 o'Clock P.M.

PART II.

OLD LETTERS & JOURNALS;

My Dear Turnbull,

The story I told to your wife a few evenings ago is perfectly correct, but if you wish to have it in detail, it is as follows :—

My father's family hailed from a Scottish estate, which had been in their possession for 26 generations. My father went into trade as a London merchant, but died at the early age of 38, leaving my mother with three children—two sisters and myself, the youngest born. In an evil hour she married again, and her second husband soon scattered her little stock of money, and was thrown into Whitecross prison for debt. At this place he met with a Mr. Gardener, who, for some purpose, wished to adopt a little boy of my age, and some bargain was made between them about myself. Some months after my stepfather had left the prison I had been put to bed one night, when Mr. Gardener came for me. I was dressed and taken away by him in the "dickey" of a four-horse coach to a house near New Cross, then quite in the country, where in an upper room a lady was lying upon a bed. As we entered she rose and took me on her knee, called me darling and caressed me. My age was probably about five years at this time. In a day or two I was sent to a neighbouring preparatory school. I fretted a little for my mother, but on the whole I was tolerably happy. After a few months stay, I was permitted to go home and see my family. I had been told that in future I should be called Edward Gardener, and the lady and gentleman my mamma and papa. Of course I gave a very satisfactory account of my quarters at New Cross. My mother was satisfied, and then I returned to my adopted parents. In a few months I left the school, and Mr. and Mrs. Gardener appeared to get into difficulties. A Major Haswell, the lady's father, had occasionally visited the house. The old gentleman took some notice of me, and would often walk up and down the room and teach me my tables. In his visits now, however, he always appeared very angry. After a while they ceased, and the family appeared approaching starvation. For weeks together we had an insufficiency of food, faring almost exclusively on potatoes and red herrings. My clothing was neglected and I went without shoes. I was frequently beaten by the lady and frightened by figures dressed up in the garden, while the man would sometimes give me port wine until I was ill. He would frequently swear and teach me filthy songs. Matters grew worse, and finally the lady went away. One night Gardener and two men accompanied by a boy older than myself came to the house. They heaped up a large fire, brought up a quantity of port wine on a tray, and sat up all night drinking until they were all drunk, including the boy, who became very sick. Towards five or six o'clock in the morning the men and the boy went away and Gardener went to bed. Shortly afterwards a knock came at the door, and he bade me speak out of the window to the man and say there was nobody in the house except myself, which I did. The man at the door replied "that no one would have left a child in a house alone, and that what I said was a lie." He persisted, and at length Gardener arose and admitted him. He proved to be an officer of some kind, and immediately arrested Gardener, leaving me in the house alone. The house looked over a dreary waste of level fields—the weather was very boisterous, and the banging of the doors and roaring of the wind acting upon nerves reduced by bad living and a sleepless night nearly destroyed my senses during the long day, during which I tasted no food. In the evening, two women, formerly servants in the house, came to me. One left immediately, the other remained and insisted upon my going to bed. I do not think I slept, and after some hours I heard repeated knocking at the door of the house. While I was dressing to go down to the door the remaining woman staggered into my room, and fell prone in a complete state of drunkenness. I admitted the knocker, who was Major Haswell. I do not know what was done, but I was again put to bed, and the next day there was a consultation between the Major and a brother of Mr. Gardener, evidently about the disposal of my poor little self. It was found that my stepfather had removed from his late place of residence and could not be found, and it was decided that I should be sent to the workhouse. Mrs. Gardener returned to the house where she was met by her husband, who appeared in an officer's uniform; meanwhile most of the goods in the house were removed. During the few days that matters were in this miserable condition, an old woman, formerly a servant in the house, seemed to take a great interest in me, and questioned me as to what relations I had and where they lived. I happened to remember the address of an aunt, to whom she immediately sent, which resulted in my mother being informed of the probability of my becoming an inmate of the workhouse. She immediately came to me, and I shall never forget the sensation of joy at seeing her enter the door. So ended the episode, which I give to you as it occurred, leaving to your imagination to guess the why and wherefore of the whole matter, which has always been beyond me entirely. I have left out a thousand little particulars of the period, which I will tell you when next we meet over the walnuts and the wine—

Always yours,

D. S.

CAMDEN STATION, *27th May*, 1852.

The haste, the noise, the anger, the heap of papers, the earnest words of command, attendant on the earning of my daily bread, have past over somewhat earlier than usual to-day, and I turn with refreshing pleasure to the clear page on which I have determined to mark a few words, of my usual free and easy style, to my dear brother *Reuben. If my thoughts could but be daguerreotyped, how often you would have a long epistle. You would have my notions of everything I see and hear, and, instead of blowing me up for my silence, you would send me a piteous appeal to desist. Strange to say, nothing new or remarkable comes within my ken, but straight I set it down that I will send you a description of it, and then time flies and I never do it, yet I dream the same again, often and often. What spell have you cast over me? Is it my vanity you flatter? or is it that I feel certain I may be quite unrestrained to you? that if, in the frolicsome gambols of my mind, the slender garment of prudence which it wears, falls on one side and reveals some evil beneath, you will not be severe in your criticism.

2nd June, 1852.—I was called away from the above, as I often am when I intend to write to you.

We have Whitsuntide fair at Chalk Farm. What an awful celebration of the coming of the Holy Ghost. The poor ignorant slaves of society go through the process of "enjoying themselves" on these occasions; that is, they drink bad beer by the gallon, and struggle in crowds to get it from the 'bar,' as though life and death were at stake; they swing in perilous machines till they scream with nausea, and think it fine fun when the man wont "stop the ship," and relieve some agonised wretch. They dance in close rooms on perhaps six square inches of space, and fight on the same extent of ground. Smoke also they do, like funnels. Husbands and wives enter freely into these delights, dragging their poor little ones through it all. Old women refresh their aged bodies in the same way, and forget that they are old: one fell out of a swing yesterday and cut her eye out—poor old creature! Young men and maidens go into the pleasureable vortex, like mad; and oh, for the maidens! Many a misery dates its commencement from the visit to the fair. Little boys, too—they do enjoy the fair —yea, without the beer or the dancing; they may go to the extent of a fight, now and then, but they principally feed on the clowns at the shows—*that* is their weakness. They admire the whitened degraded wretch twisting his body and thrusting out his poor

---

*A nick name in allusion to Reuben and Joseph in Scripture

tongue for sixpence a day, and think how hard they will try to imitate him when they go home to their dirty miserable domiciles. Could you accompany the little ragged fellows to their resting places, you would find them going through the performance on their beds, or dreaming of the glorious fair in that sleep which blesses youth under all circumstances. Could you see them in the park the next day you would find them throwing somersaults and studying to be clowns. What is the age about, that some better object of ambition is not placed before them. Further on in life we shall find these boys very bad men, and, as this sort of character is much on the increase among us, is it not probable that in time they will give the nation a strong tinge of their colour? We are making way for their operations with such propositions as universal suffrage, &c. What will be the end of it all? I wish I could be quite sure that I have no responsibility in the matter. I am only a poor clerk; surely it is a small speck of blame that will fall to my share when the Nation is judged! * * *

I dined at the Freemasons' Tavern a short time since, along with the Licensed Wittlers. The dinner was hot and excellent, and the wine good,—so were the songs. Sir Henry Meux made a speech. I sipped my wine, and enjoyed the noisy scene. The sight was like some painting I have seen; some Roman or Grecian banquet. If I were learned I would quote the subject in Greek or Latin, and tell you the artist's name. The room where we dined is very large and handsomely decorated, and is capable of accommodating about four hundred people. The good feeling and the wine had a happy effect on my state of mind, and I dreamed pleasantly of the last time I was in that place. The tables for the moment disappeared, sweet music filled the air of the ball room, and youth and beauty shone at every turn. Merry laughter and many twinkling feet kept sweet accord with the pleasing strains of music. The figure of L—— in purple velvet and white fur is there, and a pale young 'feller' waltzes by her side. Lovers and jealousy are there, too; little they know how soon death will come between them!—fair forms, how soon to fade!—pure hearts, full of hope, how soon to lose their freshness!—cloudless brows and rosy cheeks, how soon to pale and bear the impress of Care's cruel feet! My dream was disturbed, for here the waiter upset a dish over my new coat, and a Licensed Wittler blessed his eyes. And now, while I write this, where are the waiters and the Wittlers? That company will never meet the same again. Where will they be when next I enter that Hall? Where are the people who met at the Ball? Where? Now scattered never to meet again on earth!

14th June, 1852.—I went last evening to what is called a Puseyite church. It stands in Munster Square, formerly York Square—a place better known than respected. I like the fine stained-glass windows, the tasteful gaslights, the ample room provided to kneel, the division of the men from the women, the soul-elevating music, and the general unanimity of the congregation in responding; but I don't like the removal of the Commandments and Belief from the Communion table, and the substitution of a painted veil of gold, with a cross in the middle, and a candle burning on each side, for show, and not for light, towards which all the devotions appear to be made. I don't like this, because I think Christians, aged or youthful, will get wrong through the practice. I don't like the universal rising when the clergymen and choristers come through an iron gate, as though out of a monastery, into the church, in long procession. This savours of Popery, and is just getting a little too far in that direction, without much being gained in other respects. Davie is jealous of too much homage being paid to you parsons, it leads both priest and people into error. I miss the prayer for God's blessing, in the pulpit, before the sermon, and the prayer after it. There is a shade too much bowing also, although I should not mind it if it were not done towards the rather gaudy communion table at the end of the church, so pointedly. The clergyman—Mr. Stuart, I think—preached a sermon on public worship, and made a very good case out for the better conducting of the church services, but he defended nothing to which feel an objection. I think I shall enjoy the evening service occasionally.

15th June, 1852.—Have you seen the summer anywhere down your way? He hasn't called here this season. Mr. Rains absented himself in the early part of the year, for some months, sending, in his stead, a very disagreeable and windy person, called East. East came from a cutting quarter, a keen fellow, and a great favourite with the coal trade. He wasn't at all popular here, though; so Rains came down upon us himself, about a month since; and, by jingo, he doesn't appear to be going yet. My wife put a lot of "ornaments for yer fire stove" in our grate about six weeks since, expecting Summer, knowing that that gentleman objected to a fire; and here we are, sneaking into the kitchen, among big pots, black beetles, and crickets, at every opportunity.

26th June, 1852.—This week I have been engaged at a trial in the Court of Exchequer. The Achili case was on in the 'Bench,' but you could not have poked so much as your nose into the place, it was so crowded.

Did you ever see a Baron of the Exchequer in full costume? The Barons were going about in great state yesterday, and I had much difficulty in keeping a serious face. I begin to think that they go about for the purpose of making poor witnesses laugh, in order to commit them for contempt; the shocking old guys being so short of work, now that the County Courts give the people cheap law.

What do you think of the Achili case? Oh, you parsons are terrible fellows! Before the *Times* issued its late article—before, mind!—I arrived at the same conclusion, viz., that the exhibition of two christian priests ripping each other up in this way is a fine bone for the grinning infidel and the sneering scoffer. It strikes me, also, that the Roman Catholics will be losers, not only of the trial, but of proselytes. In exposing this man, Achili, they have exposed their own system; and the holding up to the light of the awful power of the priests, the fearful and uncontrolled establishment of the Inquisition, the possible result of sending a daughter to confess to a man vowed to celibacy, and all the paraphernalia of the matured but objectionable system of the Roman Church, will do more to frighten the English people away than would even the preaching of a Robert Turnbull at St. Paul's Cross! Talk of High Church! To hear and see all we do of the Romish Church just now, is enough to make us turn Ranters, and yet how much the ages owe to the grand old Church.

Last night a Good's train broke down a few miles from here. It's a strange sight to see a lot of men, and fire and lights, and bales, and broken waggons, and clouds of steam, reflecting the light like the cloud which led the Israelites, suddenly dropped down into the silent country, where a few moments before the stars shone calmly down on stillness, save when the nightingale twittered to its mate or the light wind rippled the quiet stream. In the mysterious workings of the awful Providence which governs the earth and its inhabitants, how strangely linked together are great events and small! matters remote and unconnected with us, apparently, often become of urgent consequence to us ere long. Could we look into futurity, how different would our feelings be! When one of our carpenters went to bed last night; when he supped with his wife and made his arrangements for the morrow, and his promises for the bright summer days; when he caressed his little-ones and thought of his future age and their manhood; when, let us hope, he knelt in prayer for his daily bread, and forgiveness for his sins; could his guardian angel have whispered in his ear that in few moments an event would occur miles away which would cause his immediate death, that to-morrow for him would be no more, that no summer sun would ever shine on his living brow again, that he had kissed the sweet lips of his darlings for the last time, that his heart, which so lately warmed with love and pride and hope for the future, would never kindle with an old father's admiration, that he needed to pray, but oh! not for the bread of this life; had these sentences been uttered, think you the man would have believed them? No! the improbability would have exceeded his awe at the fearful prophecy. Yet, when sleep reigned in his house a knocking came and summoned him to death. The accident near Harrow rendered it necessary to forward assistance from Camden, and several of the carpenters were called up. One poor fellow missed his footing while getting into the train and was killed on the spot. He has left a wife and large family.

28th June, 1852.—At the Puseyite Church yesterday morning an alarming sermon from a man with a nasal twang: a few hard knocks and a short round; sinners down—as the pugilists have it.

At the conclusion of the service, before the prayer for the Church Militant, a number of gentleman go round with little red velvet bags and collect the 'one thing needful,' while the clergyman reads the encouraging passages from Scripture appointed for the purpose. All very correct and proper; but the tinkling of the sixpence, the unoccupied air of the congregration, and the dropping pauses between the sentences read by the Priest, have a strange effect. It is just the time that Mrs. Sloe, the tea-dealer's wife, reckons up the new summer toggery of Mrs. Alum, the baker's wife,—when Julia Languish takes the opportunity of ascertaining whether that dear fellow with the slight moustache is in his place. The proper way, I fancy, is to do what the young lady with the gold 'kivered' prayer book appears to do, namely, to kneel in silent prayer; but she throws herself down on the hard floor with such force that her knees must suffer: and can anyone pray in pain?

In the evening to St. James's Chapel, Hampstead Road, Mr. Stebbing did not preach, but a young man edified us with a beautiful sermon from the sentence, "But thou has kept the good wine until now." It was a fervid, comforting, discourse, touching the heart with the love and hope of christianity and showing God's ultimate good to his creatures, though here they might be visited with sorrow and affliction. It was likely to soften the hardened, to win the wavering, and soothe the troubled; and a few sound truthful arguments, candidly and entreatingly expressed, as from one man to another, completed the effective address.

29th June, 1852.—Eliza and Mrs. Hutton went to Barnet yesterday, so I took the opportunity of stealing off to the theatre, to see a much talked-of piece called the "Vampire." There are no end of ghosts in it, which caused me to whistle a great deal as I came up our dark lane on my way home. I saw a fight in Oxford Street,—up and down, hard blows, blood, and curses ground between the teeth, a scream, a crowd, and a policeman, as if from the bowels of the earth, stood between the combatants, who dropped their arms sulkily to the Majesty of the law. One drunken non-combatant became strongty pot-valiant when there was no fear of a fight being allowed. "Show me," said he. "show me a man, and I'll fly into him like a 'hevil genus!'" So home to bed.

I have just been to see Mrs. Walker, the widow of my poor friend the Locomotive Manager here, of whom I wrote to you some time since. A pretty good collection has been made for her, but with her large family it is a small allowance. She will be confined in August and add another fatherless child to the number. At best, the attention of kind-hearted friends but ill supplies the father's place; and the troublesome advice of well meaning persons perplexes and mocks the bruised heart. She is a very pure-minded and upright woman, and a credit to Auld Scotland. God will not desert her.

I am just about to shut up. Another day has rolled away, and, like the waves of the receding tide leaving the beach revealed, another multitude of sins, equal in number to the grains of sand on the shore, are recorded. Why does the earth remain? Why are men born to destruction? A breath of His will would crumble up the rolling globe, teeming with living things, and scatter it into space, as bursts the soap-and-water globule from the boy's tobacco pipe and is no more seen. Incomprehensible scheme! how profound are thy mysteries! how perplexing thy revelations! how immeasurably mighty must be thy Maker, the vast and unfathomable God! O puny earth,—yet great and inexhaustibly wonderful earth! And man—how insignificant! Wondering over all, daring to approach even to the Great First Cause of all,—ungovernable, restless,—flows the never-dying thought. Reasoning, questioning comparing, praying, yet sinning —Free Essence! Eternal Soul! Beautiful gift of the all-bountiful Creator! Why, oh! why art thou not ever stainless? What unseen end is accomplished by thy association with corruption and evil? Patience! It is told us that Eternity will come, and time and sin will be no more. Beauty and grace, and pure and holy love will be in Heaven. Bright Heaven! a home of never fading light and everlasting happiness, where glory, untainted by ambition or death, will shine on all for ever.

July 7th, 1852.—I have been very gay lately. Last week we had Mrs. Hutton and two lady friends stopping with us. They went to Gravesend one day, and T. L. and I joined them in the afternoon. On my journey down I left the "Meteor" steamboat about two minutes before she saved the passengers from the unfortunate "Duchess of Kent." One of our people whom I left on board saw it all, and described the scene as awful in the extreme. On Saturday I went to Grays on a visit until Monday. My host introduced me to an old lady, the proprietress of an inn, her son, and three pretty black-eyed daughters. The old woman is quite a character, and tells very funny stories of life when she was young, fifty years ago.

Coming home in the boat on Monday, I talked with some soldiers, and was highly edified with a "gent" with moustaches, who boasted of the superiority of the travelling arrangements on the Continent, and wanted to know "Wart we were detayned foh." He twiddled his hair and showed his ring—an immense one—and behaved as became a fop; and I was enraged to see a beautiful fair-haired, rosy, blue-eyed girl evidently admiring him, and smoothing her face and furbelows to be admired in return.

To an evening concert, with the girls, at the Beethoven rooms. Good music. These entertainments seldom pay, I believe. They are usually half-filled with orders, and are mostly intended to get up a name for some singer who wants to be considered a rising man. Mr. F. B. was the aspirant in this case, and we four paid nothing. It is very nice to wear white kids and sit with scented folks in a beautiful drawing room, to hear sweet sounds from pretty women and well-dressed men. I like to take the scene into my fancy, and believe that all the people present are really what they seem—human butterflies— whose hands are never soiled, whose faces never frown, whose lips are always pure; and not Alum the baker, and Sloe the grocer, and Hookit the swindler, and David the clerk, with their cleaned gloves and greased heads. That the ladies are all angelic as they appear, and that no struggle has occurred to get the pretty brooch or the gay ribbon; but let us spare them! they are so much better than men, that they are angelic comparatively. Home late. Felt the appeal to my gallantry in my pocket, being the only gentleman with three ladies; which cabs *is* expensive.

7th July, 1852.—This night by the death bedside of poor S. He was a strong fine man, with good hope of a long life. We liked him for his bass songs and friendly disposition, and forgave him his prosy stories about his native town, Manchester, which he, poor man, considered a model city. Some time ago he had lodgings in some house where he picked up a woman and married her, and, when too late he discovered her to have been a disreputable character. She soon evinced a partiality for spirits and pawned his property. He, however, in some measure reformed her. and kept her with him. Disgusting to tell, the near approach of his death imbued her with a desire to get hold of what little money he had, to indulge in her propensity while he lay gasping for life on a sick bed. Finally, after a day of drunkenness, she endeavoured to get his watch from beneath his pillow; and it so exasperated the dying man that he rushed up from the bed and ran after her into the street. With much difficulty we got him to bed again, and obtained from her the watch and some of his money, which he placed in the custody of a neighbour. Assured by the doctor of the impossibility of his recovery, I entreated S. to think no more of his earthly possessions, and bade him look for pardon and hope where alone it can be found,—and may God consecrate the words which were offered by my unworthy lips, to the salvation of his soul! May he grant me in my last hour that hope and consolation with which I fain would have impressed this poor man!

9th July, 1852.—Here's a pretty woman with a baby wants me—very ominous—with a sweet smile too. Bless me! It was Mrs. P. Now Mrs. P. is the wife of Mr. P., a young clerk, a gentlemanly young man, with few influential friends. He lost his situation some three months ago and has been pinched very hard by "short commons." He told Mr. Mills, in confidence, that a porter's place would be acceptable, if it were in the country, out of sight of those who had seen him better off. Poor fellow! So we have managed to put him on as office porter at Watford, and he and she are so overjoyed and so thankful, and think us so good to grant them a pass and to free their goods—scanty sticks, poor dears—as if it cost me or Mr. Mills anything. It is pleasant; no, altogether it is *not* a pleasant thing to receive undeserved gratitude. One feels somehow an impostor; and yet it is a comfort to behold new-found happiness.

When in Oxford Street yesterday evening, one of our people and I were boyish enough to go into a show to see a wonderful lady with a beard and whiskers. She introduced herself politely as a native of Geneva, twenty-one years of age. Her neck was white, and unmistakably a woman's, but her face looked about thirty-five years old. Hair grew round her cheeks and chin, and some ladies present pulled it; it was evidently genuine. She wore a gold watch and a black satin dress, and a wonderful head-dress of diamonds (?) "Laydes and gent'men," said she, "I em vaisey mush oblige. My bebby is at de door." The baby at the door was a beauty, but I don't believe in *it*.

10th July, 1852.—Here's a letter come requesting me to state the condition of Mr. Jack L's. health, and whether I think he is eligible for assurance, and begging me to unfold my inmost opinion, in confidence, to the Secretary of the concern. Well, what shall I say? Jack is a strong fellow; he can eat—rather! he can jump or run, and on a pinch could ram his head through a cheese or a grindstone. Yes, Mr. Secretary, unless you are a very strong man, Jack will see us both out, sir; we shall be down in the dust and evaporated, before Jack gives up. Lor, Sir Sec! you and I may help to eke out old Jack at last. He may smell us or eat us, through some of nature's strange transfers, and get us into his blood somehow; and who knows whether that won't set him a-thinking of us—dead and gone—and soften him; for somewhere about him there *are* tears and soft feelings, although he's rough now—very; and so we may do something for *him*, dead, though we do nothing for anybody living. And believe me, brother quill-driver, our doings for Jack, or anyone else, here, are as much a mystery, and the work of the Great Governor, as the silly conceit I have just uttered about our probable doings hereafter.

12th July, 1852.—Emily and Eliza and I went to the Marionette Theatre on Saturday evening. The Adelaide Gallery forms a pretty little house; but oh, for poor Punch and Judy, whom the Police Act endeavoured to annihilate! They are infinitely superior to this affair. The marionette puppets have dreadful convulsions, especially when they walk, and the audience continually make mistakes as to the person speaking. The voices behind the scenes are out of proportion. One curious effect I observed. After looking at the performance an hour or two the eye becomes unable to form an estimate of the real size of the figures. The scenes, tables, chairs, decorations, etc., being all in proportion, there is no difficulty in imagining the things as large as life, and people go away with different notions of the height and size of them. Emily thinks they were nearly as large as life. Eliza says they were about the height of a girl twelve years old. Mrs. Livock and John, who have been to see them, say about half the size of life; and I myself am confident they do not exceed two feet. This may seem stupid, but it is true.

To church at St. Mark's; Mr. Galloway not back yet. I understand he has lost his wife, and is gone for change to the seaside. An appeal is made to defray the expenses of doing the work while he is away. I would put down my little mite cheerfully, but I rather object to this call. What is the use of episcopacy if it cannot meet an occasion like this? Why cannot a few reserve men be kept by the richly paid bishop? Not that I wish to speak disrespectfully of the bishop, or of any of my pastors and masters, but I do protest against the reservation of so much wealth in the higher walks of the pasture, while down among the flocks, where the work is to be done, the shepherds are only kept just above starvation-point, and the flocks are often prematurely fleeced to obtain that.

13*th July*, 1852.—Last evening Mr. and Mrs. Stevenson gave a select soirée at their mansion in Regent's Park Road. The aristocracy present were the right fat and podgy Mrs. H., the long Mr. M., and the elegant and accomplished Miss M., the thin Mr. R. M., and the pretty Miss H., of Hampstead. Singing was kept up to a late hour, when a recherché supper was served, in Betsy's best style, on the two parlour tables shoved together. The amiable Mr. H. attended in his spectacles, and performed *Lucy Neal*, with variations, on the violin. The last reveller from Chalk Farm Tavern was turned out by the landlord, as the party emerged from Montrose House amid the music of much laughter and many shakings of hands. There is no truth in the report that Mr. M. kissed Miss M. while they were looking for Miss M.'s parasol in the passage, although it is generally considered that the worthy host acted very improperly in carrying away the light at the precise juncture, particularly as the young couple will be married in February next, and ought not to require kissing at all, considering what a lot of that sort of thing they will have to undergo then.

I have been to Eliza's doctor in Finsbury Square to ascertain the real state of her health. He says the air we live in is impure. I think he is a humbug. He has ordered Eliza to Ramsgate immediately, and says she will soon be well there. The doctor told me I looked as though I lived in bad air, and that I confirmed his previous notion. He added, however, that I had a strong constitution.

What an awful place is the waiting-room of a physician! One cannot help feeling that every person there has some dreadfully bad place under his or her clothes. Wounds and sores appear to surround one, and a little imagination would make you sure that the apartment smelt of disease. I fancy the feeling is something akin to that of those who "passed by on the other side," in the case of the man who fell among thieves. No doubt the lady who stared at me was wondering what I had the matter with me—whereabouts the bandages were, and whether it was the result of accident, of hereditary disorder, or of personal neglect. I was glad when the man in plush responded to my silver key and showed me in to the medical man. Plush thinks himself half way towards being a doctor; he speaks of "our patients," "our fees," "our busiest time," in the worst English, it is true, but with the tone of a man convinced that he has had a hand in the cures; and, in many cases, I believe the grammar is the only difference between Jeames and his master.

15th July, 1852.—One of our teams killed a poor little child, about eight years of age, yesterday. It died on the spot; and so an angel went up to Heaven leaving its mantel of grief hanging heavily on its parents.

Sauntering from dinner just now I paused where two houses are being built, when the foreman and an English labourer had a few words, more emphatic than elegant. A paddy from the opposite job, sung out "Don't swear," which injured the dignity of the brave Englishman, and he forthwith walled across and fetched Paddy a punch on the nose; but the fall he got immediately must have relieved him of a little wind. Up he rose and again assailed the Irishman, immersing the Emerald Isle in deluges of sanguinary expressions. Englishmen always do throw poor Pat's country in his face in a quarrel. Again the bold Englisher went down a "buster"; when a little man with a bullet head—I hope he wasn't an Englishman—came behind Paddy and smote him a dig in the ear that would have polished off such a man as your friend Davey entirely. This was the signal for a general scrimmage " Hooroo, ye devils " was heard on all sides. As I was the only impartial person present I sheered off to a deferential distance, and in about a quarter of an hour the storm subsided, save now and then the distant thunder of the original Englishman's voice, dying away in discontented grumbles.

* * * * * * *

By the way if you don't send me a good long letter after this I shall think I am boring you. Can't you tell me, my patriotic parson, how the country is going on—whether, because Snooks, or Leatherlungs, or Freebread is "in," the country will topple down to destruction, or because Steadycourse and Scornpraise are left out, no one can be found to govern the country? "Lor, Sir!" you should tell me; for I get bewildered between the arguments and protestations—the patriotism, the ambition, the jaw, the claptrap, and the deceit of politics. One thing often strikes me, and that is, that with nations, as with children, they may have good governors, or bad, from whom they may imbibe a something, one way or the other, but the bulk of the result will be found to be in their own nature. They are for the most part born what they will be, in spite of the straws which stand in the way.

16*th July*, 1852.—Talked to a sort of running porter, who gets his living by finding 'busses' for passengers, opposite the Mansion House. "Such a living as it is," said he,—adding "but I could yarn more, yellowmen, if it warnt for my 'sperit.' I hev got sich a sperit. Now, if you hadn't answered to my satisfaction, no more you'd a had out o' me. I never axes twice—I can't—it goes agen me summuz. Now, there's that cove over there—t'other side o' the way,—there's him, as is at it now. He makes a tidy thing of it—five or six bob a night. He reglar insults people. I hate sich mean ways. Here's a Ampstead bus, sir,—thankee, sir—good night, sir, and thankee for me."

17th July, 1852. Detained at Bayswater for several hours by a most awful storm,—such blue grinning lightning and such bursting clattering thunder!

19th July, 1852.—I went to Southall on Saturday night, on a visit to a very delightful family. Mr. G. is surveyor of the roads under the Metropolitan Commissioners. He has a nice house, keeps two horses, a four-wheel and a gig, and has a splendid garden, full of glorious flowers and fruit, with fountains and nooks and arbours,—a large farm-yard, a field, and a piece of ground for wurzel and other stuff for two cows, all laid out in good order, so that you may stroll about and enjoy yourself for hours. There are several boys, from eight to eighteen years old, and two daughters, one twelve and the other twenty; and they are the most amiable and loving young folks that I have seen for many a day. The boys wait on the girls like gallants, and on their mother, whose every wish is anticipated. She is an amiable woman and has been a beauty. A few years ago she lost one of her legs by an accident and she wears a cork one, and the tenderness that has grown out of that sorrow is beautiful to see. Thus good continually arises out of evil,— adversity and affliction purify the soul. The old gentleman is so hospitable. He makes his visitors eat and drink, routs them out of bed in the morning, and shows in a thousand ways his great kind heart.

We heard an excellent sermon from the incumbent of Norwood Green Church. I felt much of the discourse as applicable to myself, and made some solemn resolutions; but if you only knew what a weak man I am, how prone to evil, how yielding and unenergetic, you would pity me. I sometimes long for one hour of sincere repentance and belief in the saving atonement of our blessed Redeemer, and then to quit this world of temptation for ever. For who would live but that it is the will of Him who will dispose of us hereafter? May He grant me grace to keep me in the right path, to resist evil and myself, (who am full of evil,) and take me into His Kingdom, in His own time, when this fight, so inglorious to me hitherto, shall cease.

26th July, 1852.—On Saturday evening I went to Harrow to reconnoitre for a house, as I intend, in the course of a year or two (D.V.), to remove thither, in order that James shall be qualified for admittance into the Harrow School, and also for the sake of Eliza's health. There is plenty of ground marked out for building, and it is a fine place. Such a magnificent view from the churchyard. "Ah!" said the sexton to me, "There's where old Byron had his tea-things many a brave day," pointing to some unfortunate person's tombstone, which has been chipped almost all away by the enthusiastic Britishers and Yankees, because Lord Byron used to recline upon it and contemplate the view of the country. The poor sexton walked away in disgust when he found I had no inclination to listen to his story nor to fork out sixpence.

28th July, 1852.—Last night amongst a lot of cricketing gentlemen, who are mad for bats and belts and leggings and flannel jackets, to the great profit and satisfaction of Mr. C., who teaches them to play and supplies their little requirements. He is a tanned shady-faced man, with white whiskers and a nose which appears to have had the gristle taken out for the convenience of cricketing, and he evidently considers cricket to be as important a subject of discourse as free trade or the Protestant cause. He talks solemnly about it, as though there were more in it than the world could be prevailed upon to believe. C. harangued the club last night and strongly recommended the social glass as a good thing to "keep your men together." The good man strengthened his precept by an energetic practice, and although he profoundly announced several times that he had had his "dose," yet he yielded to his inclination and suffered himself to be persuaded into another glass. What a terrible thing that drink is! If intoxicating liquors could be utterly abolished what a happiness it would be to the world!

19th October, 1852.—When shall I cease to tell you that we are very busy? When? Ah! when? Will no one leave me a fortune? Shall I always ply the pen to keep my wife and piccaninnies? I suppose so; and a good dispensation too, I feel sure. So my hand must shake, and my noddle tremble, and shuffling limbs support my bended back and silvered head before I can tell you that I am released from toil. Well, we *are* busy this time. The gold-diggers have found the treasure and raised their voices to such a tune that the mighty sound rings through all the workshops of old England. The wax, and the thread, and the leather combined into boots and shoes by the bootmakers of Northampton come up in tons daily, to be shipped; thousands of tons of cotton goods from the clicking, snorting factories of Lancashire pour through our sheds (to be shipped); Sheffield cutlery comes from *Birmingham*, in bewildering quantities, to be shipped; Staffordshire crates, Coventry ribbons and watches, Worcestershire carpets, canvas and linen from Scotland, and woollen bales from Yorkshire teem into the station to be tumbled out and shipped; while the salt provisions, biscuits, wines and spirits for the voyages are astounding. Then, to keep the pot boiling (down), we are obliged to hurry hides to be tanned, and no end of other stuff to tan them, and the bark off all the trees in England, I am sure, to help. Square bales of foreign wool are hauled from the dark holds of ships and bundled into Yorkshire; stag horns, elephants' tusks, flax, ironstone, oil, to be manufactured; and tea, sugar, wine, beer, fish, flour, corn, tons on tons, to feed the manufacturers; with guano to grow their vegetables, and bonnets, perfumery, pianos, furniture, and toys for their wives and families. And all this besides the meat and potatoes in hundreds of tons weekly, and nine thousand head of animals to feed the cockneys who keep the account of all these mighty movings, with six hundred thousand tons of coal to help to light the fires to cook the grub. Oh, dear me! Silk (raw) to Macclesfield, and manufactured silk up from the same; lace from Nottingham; glue, grindstones, gum, gun-barrels, bottles, anchors, and American clocks, gutta percha, ice and iron bedsteads, grease, grates, blacking bottles, garden seats, machinery, bobbins, needles in awfully heavy little packages, bees wax, blankets from Witney, cables and clogs, butter and buttons, pitch and pumice-stone, cannon balls, reaping hooks, and soldiers' clothing. Then it is the heaviest hop season ever known, and the tightly stuffed pockets are rolling in upon us unrelentingly, until pile on pile is stacked up to wait for waggons and tarpaulins, which cannot be obtained for them in consequence of the unprecedented increase of our trade.

23rd October, 1852.—Crowded, and crammed, and jammed, here we are again this morning, and the rain coming down like a water-spout, and a coal engine has just run into the broadside of the down mail, sending the lot to smithereens and blocking our line, so that the goods train can't go out. Nobody hurt but the driver. If you could only see the débris, you'd say it was a miracle.

27th October, 1852.—Swift has just been asking us to meet J. at his house and make it up; and so we go on unto our lives' end, as thousands have gone on before us. What a breadth and importance we attach to our own little span! How we smile and philosophise over the lives of those who have preceded us! "All the world's a stage,"—but all the men and women are very fond of thinking themselves the *audience*.

28th October, 1852.—What clever writers are bursting into print with letters to the *Times!* One sapient individual proves even too much. He first says that the Companies have long known that one accident costs more than the expenses of an efficient staff for a year, and then adds that, for the sake of *economy*, the Companies prefer an occasional accident to keeping an efficient staff, because it costs less. Wonderful man! The fact of the matter is, that the prosperity of the country has so suddenly and so vastly increased, that the railways cannot sufficiently expand to receive it. They had scarcely recovered from the Exhibition inundation when this flood of unexpected traffic came upon them. The people, by their representatives, forced the railways into the lowest possible fares and rates, by allowing competition; and, unless they forfeited their dividends, it would be impossible for the Companies to keep a large reserve of plant and trained officers to meet such an unprecedented influx of traffic as the present. They *did* keep every department full-handed before other lines were allowed to go into their districts in violation of their vested rights. As far as the road is concerned, our one railway is ample for the traffic of all the districts it covers. It is the spare engines and experienced hands of which we are deficient, and these time only can enable the abused but anxious directors to supply. Some grocer who mixes red lead with his cayenne, and takes an apprentice, whose marrow and bones he uses up for seven years without a penny payment, and commits daily other tricks of trade, having more ink than brains, and a *cacoethes scribendi*, humanely suggests the mulcting the poor station clerks, or the forcing a director to ride on the frame of each engine. Witty and intelligent person! If by his adulterations, which, poor man, he would say the competition in trade obliged him to practice against his conscience, he could scrape together sufficient to become a railway director, he would change his tune to that of the grinding, cheese-paring, penny-wise and pound-foolish description of man who now and then gets upon the Board, but whose illiberal policy is mostly kept under by the better sense of the other directors. There! having disgorged my bile, I'll go to dinner.

16th November, 1852.—Not a word to you for ten days. Well! floods and things have so "served us out" that really one has felt like Job. No sooner has one bespattered guard told his tale of disaster by flood and field, than another man rushes up to announce another stoppage. Kensington under four feet of water; West London line damaged; Bedford branch flooded and impassable; Poplar station submerged; Peterborough branch blocked by the surging waters; Oxford branch tunnel fallen in; and Kilsby main-line tunnel queer. Midland viaduct washed away, and a bridge on the Trent Valley line ditto. Rugby and Stamford line under water, South Staffordshire branch also swamped, with a multitude of minor mischances. Our neighbours, too, have been as badly visited. The Great Western, Great Northern, and Eastern Counties, have all been more or less shut up by the rolling waters. Can you tell your poor lay brother-clerk what it all means? Is the clerk of the weather selling his rain off at a ruinous sacrifice? or are the elements weeping for the death of England's hero? If the latter they have the water laid on from the main, as Sam Weller says.

26th November, 1852.—Two hundred and thirty loads of cattle and goods came into this station within three-quarters of an hour on Saturday night,—such a job! Talk of managing people, or anything else, in moving masses! What use would the great Duke have been at Camden? We delayed the express, and the passengers enunciated their opinions of us. Who cares? Let'em get out and do it themselves—that's all. One of the passengers told me a joke, by way of relief. When they arrived at Leighton the porter sang out, as usual, "Lay-tun! Lay-tun!" which a young fellow, afflicted with wit, said was exasperating in the extreme, considering that it was enough to know-that the train *was* a "late'un," without the fact being bawled into their ears by a porter hired and liveried for the purpose.

7th December, 1852.—I am taking a dip now and then into those beautiful lays of the Scottish Cavaliers, and I am on those occasions carried up above the present altogether. I soar above Camden Station, and dream in that lovely cloudland of romance.

* * * * * *

How about your income tax of fivepence-farthing in the pound? What do you now think of Dizzy? Some of our men are emigrating; and who would not do so in their circumstances? The hundred pound per annum men are the strength and sinews of the mercantile world. They are also just the men who will emigrate and do well. There never was a more unwise measure than to put such a heavy tax on to poor struggling chaps with few comforts and many children. I rub against these men (I have been one of them single, and I may be one of them married some day,—I don't deserve to be so well off as many of them), and I know what they have to bear in a place like London, and how well they bear it; hoping for ever, and being careful of their duty, and their clothes, and their "kids," in the meanwhile. It is wrong to take these poor fellows' pence. It is an effectual plan to prevent the children getting education, and the ability to see how their rulers are exempted from paying legacy duty, &c.

9th December, 1852.—I have just been at the Cattle Show, on business. I am happy to say that all my important trains of cattle are in for to-day. Whether I shall get over the next three heavy days, without delaying the passenger trains and incurring discredit, I cannot tell. It is a lottery. Our place is small, and the overwhelming trains of goods and cattle come pouring in.

One needs a voice of thunder, and wings, so as to be at all points in a little time.

21st December, 1852.—Here is one of my men who has taken his time-piece, on the sly, to the maker's, who contracts for repairs. It is completely smashed. On taking a glance at the chap's proboscis, I perceive that he has had a whack on that instrument; and on calling up my memory, I do bethink me that I saw his lordship come out of a public-house early one morning last week. Now, he says that he had only been in for half-a-pint of beer, as a great exception; that the train started suddenly, and hurled him against the iron rail of his break, and that at another time a bit of iron flew up and cut his nose. What are you to do in such a case? Let him go, I suppose, and tell him to look out; pull a grave face, and bid him think of his family, and not fall into evil habits; all of which he meets by strong assertions that he has long seen the necessity of a virtuous career, and that that is why he has become such an exemplary character, the admiration of all his acquaintances, &c., &c.

22nd December, 1852.—The note of preparation sounds for Christmas. Special trains are harnessing to convey wandering sons to the fireside of old home, to carry the eye and heart from the eager pursuit of gain and distinction back to that dear place where the prayer was first learned and the precept given, there to note with tenderness the signs of increasing years in the devoted parent, the kindling manhood of the brother, and the beauty of the young sister. Steam, too, is preparing in the big engine to bring in the long Parliamentary train filled with hard-working toilers. They each arrive with a small bundle of presents for their friends; and when they get out of the train and meet Jack or Tom they shake hands,—and there's no mistake about the squeeze. The bewildering mass of turkeys, hares, geese, parcels of perishables, &c., which pour out of every incoming train is truly distracting. Clerks have to sit up all night and all day, with bread and beef in one hand, to keep up the steam, and the pen in the other, recording these substantial tokens of the love there is in the world. Turn 'em out,—here you are,—and there's more a-coming,—call 'em over,—here's no direction,—never mind,—shove him in,—what's that?—never mind,—pick up some direction,—stick it on,— fire away!

7th January, 1853.—A bullock ran off a cattle platform last night and jumped on to the main line. He trotted majestically into the tunnel, where he received a poke in the ribs from a playful passenger engine coming up. On he went, however, for about four miles, leaving four of our men panting after him far behind, and everybody here in a state of alarm about the final result. At length up came the news. The Tring train had cut the animal "to ribbons," as my foreman said. The heart was found fifty yards from the rest of the body. The whole train went over him, but only the engine and break-van were thrown off, and no one was hurt.

11th January, 1853.—Poor, weak, silly J. E., with ill health, a nervous disposition, a poor old father and mother who loved him, respectable friends, and a confiding master and patron, collected all the Company's money (about £1,000) at his station at——, took a ticket for Tring, but came on to London last Tuesday week, by the morning mail, paid the difference of fare, and then, as the political economists say, became absorbed in the population. Up to the present we have failed to find him, although I took a detective and rushed down the line, searched his lodgings, questioned his landlady (who said she had a disease of the heart and couldn't stand it), and put him in the *Hue and Cry*.

On Sunday I went to hear Dr. Pusey preach. A good practical sermon upon our besetting sins, and it might have been all copied from Bishop Taylor's "Holy Living." Dr. Pusey looks rather miserable. His hair wants combing, and his whiskers are a dirty colour, and, being scanty, have a mangey appearance. His forehead is high, but looks higher because of a slight baldness. His neck-cloth is low and he wears no collar. His nose is well-shaped and large, and his eye rather bleared— which may be from age. He appears between fifty and sixty. You can hear his voice well, but it is hard in quality, and he gives his jaw a twitch when he speaks, which is not pleasant to see.

Last night we all went to Saddler's Wells. Saw Phelps in *Henry the Fifth*. A good play is a great enjoyment. The pantomime was very good. I should think the wonderful fellows who tumble so extraordinarily, as though they had gutta-percha spines, must have devoted the whole of their existence to their "profession," and may, consequently, be unable to read or write or do anything else.

14th January, 1853.—Allow me to tell you that we have been cultivating a very peculiar breed of pig for some time past. In fact, I may say he's more peculiar than profitable; for although we have fed him with all those inviting washes in which pigs delight, consisting of the "bilings" of all the Christmas good things, with pollard and barley-meal, and many other luxuries, the creature disdains to get fat. He maintains the most delicate proportions in spite of all our efforts; and although I love the beautiful, still I like it to pay; but this pig practically uses Pistol's reply, "Base is the slave who pays"!—and so no pork have we!

20th January, 1853.—R. went to Sadler's Wells with us as gay as a lark. He was a cheerful fellow, kind-hearted, but rather extravagant. He had a nice home, seven fine children, from eighteen years old downward (for he married very young), and good prospects, while his £300 per annum as Station Master in the goods department of —— station enabled him to live comfortably in the meantime. Last week he had £416 to pay the men, and when he returned to the office after dinner he found a leaden key broken in the lock of the safe and the money gone. He closed the station gates instantly and had every person searched, but without effect. Mr. ——, the General Manager, then sent for the lock-maker, Chubb, who pronounced it impossible to open one of his locks with a pewter key, and so they suspended R., who took the accusation to heart and ran away. His wife in a day or so received a lock of his hair and some affecting words of farewell, not expressly saying that he intended suicide, but that Mr. ——'s conduct was too much to bear and he should never behold her again. Meanwhile the Guarantee Society took possession of the house and furniture. The police seized all the private letters and papers, and £10, leaving the poor woman with five-and-sixpence and all her overwhelming trouble. So perhaps he is innocent and distracted, or perhaps guilty and cunning. He is excitable enough to be half mad under the former circumstances, and talented enough to complete a robbery of the sort dexterously.

26th January, 1853.—I am glad the journal amuses you. I find it pleasant to jot down a few thoughts and occurrences at the close of the day's work. It is agreeable now and then, too, to drag out the inner man and give him a little fresh air and paper. At best he's a secret, reserved, moody, wicked fellow, hiding himself in the recesses of the heart, where he for the most part dwells, and brooding over evil thoughts; sometimes sinful and rebellious—coveting, envying, hating; and yet inconsistent—for he sometimes lies prostrate in sorrow for error—repents and prays and vows; and sometimes, too, the recollection of his own weaknesses fills him with tenderness towards his fallen fellow-creatures, and for the poor and less richly blessed than he. These are, however, but the visits of angels to his solitude and are "few and far between." For the most part impatience and anger and pride prevail; and I say, therefore, O my friend! it does him much good to look in upon him occasionally and record a few of his aspirations. So when he gazes on the written realised thought his aspect brightens and he casts the good thought on the waters of his memory, and after many days it may return to him and stay the angry word or the harsh judgment.

27th January, 1853.—So you are grumbling because you don't make Whitchurch the most Christian parish in the kingdom! You don't know what is going on under the dark surface. The grain has been cast in, and the harvest-time may come when you are far away. The floods may wash away, or rot some of it, but surely all will not be lost. The green blade may not arise in the soul until the last moments of life, and then may have such a ray of heavenly sunshine poured down upon it that in an hour the ripened ear may appear to view, before the Christian sighs away existence. Certainly no words of exhortation earnestly and prayerfully poured out to a congregation can be entirely lost. Some heart must be touched, some conscience moved—it may be to fall asleep again; but two or three such knocks must awake the sleeper.

* * * * * *

Now what is to be done with a package consigned to

"Young,"——"till called for"? because, although it is entered as "Glass, with care," an enterprising checking-clerk has discovered, through a crevice, that it contains the body of some individual deceased. It came here very early yesterday morning, and " Young " don't seem to care about coming for the glass up to this juncture, 8 p.m. After 3 a.m., when the trains are most of them gone, and the gas is turned down a little, you won't find many clerks or porters in the large dark shed, in the particular corner where the case of glass stands. "Don't stand it on end," said one of the men, when they found out the contents ; "perhaps you've got the poor fellow legs up'ards.'

28th January, 1853.—Young came for his case of glass this morning.

Beck, a poor porter in Chaplin & Horne's employ, wanted me to pass a boy down to Wolverton, our Locomotive Establishment. His boy he called him, and he was going to learn to be a mechanic. By a mere accident I learnt to-night that the boy is a very intelligent lad, and has received an excellent education at the hands of porter Beck with his eighteen shillings per week ; that he is not Beck's boy, but that the boy's father was killed on the Chester and Holyhead line, and Beck "had compassion" on him, and when he lost his father took him away and brought him up. "For as much as ye have done it, &c." Beck! glory may shine on the great here, but a glory awaits thee hereafter. Let us look to it. Let me take home a big boy, bear with his tempers, check his propensities, patiently teach him, save him from the reproaches of my wife and children in moments of thoughtlessness (and my wife should be more thoughtful than good Beck's wife), in short, take the heavy charge of him up to fourteen years of age. I'm ashamed to say I should refuse to do it, or if I did it, I should make my sins a multitude that the charity might cover them. Oh, philosopher! Cast thy pen away! Give up reflection! Turn from all the speculations on thy progress, and humbly imitate the poor man who, without education or any advantage but his eighteen shillings per week, performs an immortal good!

31st January, 1853.—I have had a long ride on the engine and am tired. You never went through a tunnel on an engine? I don't know anything more awful; although one gets so accustomed to it that it does not create any exclamation. Imagine the most utter darkness—a mighty roar beneath a vaulted roof, made by the steam, the machinery, and the action of twenty or thirty tons weight of iron rattling along at thirty miles an hour over iron rails, every joint of the rails giving out a loud sound—and then the convulsive vibration of the plate on which you stand and the rail you hold. You feel alone in the deep gloom, but yet feel that two men stand somewhere near you, and you know that all are impressed with the thought that the crack of a wheel, the fracture of a spring, a stone on the line, a loose rail, or any irregularity, would send all the iron and wood and flesh and blood and bones and fire into one wrecked heap in that dreadful place. Nothing gives me the feeling that we are helplessly in the hands of the Almighty so much as riding on an engine through a long tunnel. It is, however, pretty to see the light of the sun appear at the approaching end,—first a speck, then larger, until a small theatre is unfolded, with a natural landscape for a scene.

1st February, 1853.—We have been in a cloud here all day,—a cold, choking, dismal, dense fog. Our detonating signals, which explode like artillery when the waggons pass over them, have been booming on the station as though we were on a field of battle, and I don't know whether the place is not as dangerous as one, for we can't see ten yards, and engines and trains are flitting about in all directions, while the fog signals almost make one jump out of one's skin and into the way of danger. I have felt inclined to send messages about the station, instead of going myself. I cannot express too much admiration of the rules of war which instruct a wise general to keep himself out of danger! But the fog gets everywhere. In the open station there's an eternity of it. In the dark passage in our office you can smell it. It is in the gas-lighted room, in your hat, up your trousers' legs, and it evidently makes an attempt to get into the fire, which looks bright with indignation in consequence. Well! I want my tea, and I think I've said enough of the fog, which is a disgusting vapour made by the witches for the especial torment of railway officials.

21st February, 1853.—To-morrow the inquest sits on the

bodies of two of our coal porters who have been killed in the tunnel. The poor fellows had lain down, as is usual when two trains pass any pedestrian on the line in different directions, but instead of taking the six-feet width between the rails they took the up-line, and the low fire-box of the engine gave them no chance. One poor man was found mixed up with the machinery and frightfully mangled. He leaves a wife and five children. One of my best men has, also, crushed a finger between the buffers; and what with sickness and the frost, we are in a terrible pickle.

It is a strange thing that accidents and injuries frequently pursue one man or one family. One of the poor creatures killed in the tunnel turned the points wrong about three months ago, and made a great mess of it. Backer, a porter at Euston, was knocked and squeezed, and immediately after his return from the hospital, cured of the effects of a crush between the buffers, his arm was smashed between two carriages. He learned to write with his left hand afterwards very well. Old Woodgate, a porter here, was hurt three or more times at this station, and finally killed, while his son lost his arm a very little time after. Inspector Watts was cut to pieces by a train, and three months afterwards his son lost his ear and right arm, and was nearly killed at this place. I suppose you will say it is the effect of certain circumstances which occur in a machine like a railway, precisely or nearly similar, acting on a peculiar sort of mind, which is the same in father and son, and that the conduct of the sufferers precipitates the catastrophe.

24th, February, 1853.—Another death in the tunnel to-day— a pig this time. The poor porker, strong in his own opinion, dodged and dipped and escaped through the legs of the drovers and men on the cattle platform, who used some *pointed* and *forcible* arguments to induce him to alter his course; but he obstinately pursued his own line of policy; and while, in all probability, he was congratulating himself on the distance between him and his pursuers, an engine cut him in half.

11th March, 1853.—I went to the Great Western a few evenings ago and missed my train. Having an hour to wait I smoked a cigar and endeavoured to find out something to amuse me; and I fell in with an old face—a grey, stout, very civil, meek old man, by name Tom Calvert. Honest Tom Calvert I have seen *Bell's Life* call him. But Tom was a rogue and a hypocrite. He bought old iron of our stores department some ten years ago, kept a trotting mare, drove a large business as a fish and fruit dealer, and was well to do. His inclinations were sporting rather, and he had been a fighting man in his youth. He knew all the "fancy" and I think a few of the thieves about town. He bribed three or four of our people—G. C. who has compounded with his creditors and finally bolted, a defaulter, from his new employers; T. L., a clever fellow, who loved brandy-and-water, and who, from two or three excellent situations, has come down to be a journeyman painter; W., a decent man, who subsequently lost his berth, and now holds the situation of potman at a public-house; and M., a porter, who put his gains in the bank and is now a policeman. These men used to make Calvert's bargains worth his money. They delivered to him (for one trick) three or four tons of old iron, when he only paid for one ton. Worthy Tom Calvert married, and, getting tired of his wife, turned her off, and she went raving mad. He now keeps an oyster stall at Paddington, and talks of former days. You see that cheats really do not *always* thrive, even here.

12th March, 1853.—Wonderful men these detectives. They dont find out everything, though! One of our station-masters, whom we suspected of mal-practices, wanted a new porter, and it was thought that a detective would do well for the situation for a little time. So Mr. detective went down and joined in the fun of thieving, and other agreeable pastimes, and was considered a nice man. They, however, put the poor fellow to carry sacks of corn, which proved "too much" for a slight young London thief-taker, and so he hastened the accomplishment of his mission, and the result is that the station-master and all the porters, save one, will be discharged off-hand as soon as a staff can be organised to march into the garrison. Somehow I don't like this work. It doesn't seem English, and it is just possible that the most diabolical villainy may be practised under it some day.

* * * * * * *

Another week is closed for ever. To look forward how,

fresh and new and long the week to come appears! To look back, how brief, how unsatisfactory! Who would recall it? I have no desire to do so. Hoping and resolving, I yearn for the future alone. Some may say "Give me again the past and I will do better;" but I know I should not. When the goal is reached and the race of time draws to a close with me, I shall rejoice. Breathless, and sadly soiled with the journey, I shall rejoice to have the opportunity of casting my burden at the foot of the cross and of entering into rest.

It is a weary world. The good are secluded. One appears now and then amidst the thick battle of life, but for the most part they do not jostle on the mart. As the struggling crowd thrusts out its bruised and wounded, the good people of the world pick them up and pour oil into their wounds; but their gentle voices are not heard amid the shout and the din, the angry curses, the distorted faces, and raised arms. If they were to come into the thick of the strife, they would find such wicked, wicked men— liars, oppressors, cheats, clothed in fine cloth and respectability; grey hairs, with worldly cruel hearts; trickery marked in solemn protestation and virtuous indignation; thieves on a grand scale, witnessing against starving pilferers "for the benefit of society;" grinders of the poor "compelled by competition" to outrage their *grieved* consciences: grinders of the poor, also not so much in pocket as in unfeeling wanton words, as though no *human* heart could beat without the gold watch ticking by it, and the costly waistcoat covering it.

14*th March*, 1853.—Our clergyman is pitching into the Sunday opening of the Crystal Palace, and I am of his opinion. Who says that the masses will go to Sydenham and invigorate their bodies with fresh air and their minds by the contemplation of Nature and art? I know the British working-man too well to think that when he is "out" he will do anything so tame; and as a proof that my opinion is not singular, the public-houses within a short distance of the place are rising in value 200 or 300 per cent. The railway officials will be kept at work; the traffic in cabs will be increased; young lads and men will go on the spree; servant-girls and other young women will go there and be led astray. The artisan and his wife and bairns will drag down there and perhaps enjoy their picnic, but they will spend their boot and shoe money and get home tired. Don't tell!—as the Yankees say. At Sydenham it will be no church all day. At home there's a chance. Besides, it's a step towards the wretched state of France. Let us turn Puritans rather than that. Society would be a chaos without religion, little though its influence may sometimes appear; and without the observance of Sunday, religion cannot be worked—to use a railway term. Let us keep to the quiet Sunday. Temptations there are enough; let us make a stand against the application of capital to increase their number. Investments must be scarce indeed, when rich and quasi-moral-and-patriotic gentlemen speculate on the inclination of the people to break the Sabbath. They cannot have lived any time in the world and not know that the notion of elevating the people's minds by a Sunday trip to their great show is a humbug and a farce, and a direct violation of the Divine command to keep the Sabbath holy. I believe that the nation will incur a curse if the Sunday opening of this huge tea-garden monopoly be sanctioned; and I feel, as a humble member of the community, that to permit this desecration will be gross ingratitude for the Divine mercy towards our beloved land in sparing us the infliction of civil convulsion, and in blessing us with an unprecedented flow of prosperous commerce while the countries around us have been visited with suicidal strife, bloodshed, and annihilated liberties.

19th May, 1853.—A poor fellow, named Clarke, was knocked under the wheels yesterday, by a sudden turn of his horse, and although he had the presence of mind to save his life by rolling under the waggon, the wheels went over his foot.

The Company are going to assist my two poor widows, whose husbands were killed here. I think they will get £10 each. One of them thinks of opening a lodging-house; the other is too delicate to do much, and is a difficult subject. I am the almoner, and I feel a great deal of conceit as I walk about the poor streets visiting my patients. I should have been a precious self sufficient hypocritical humbug if I had been a parson; I know I should.

24th May, 1853.—I went to Exeter Hall last night to hear

Haydn's "Creation".—a wonderful composition. Mrs. Beecher Stowe was there, and was much applauded on entering and retiring. She appears a delicate little woman. Two clergymen accompanied her, and a black man—Uncle Tom, I suppose. She took little notice of the sensation she created; a little familiar sort of a bow, and exit.

28th May, 1853.—I went to Epsom yesterday to see the 'Derby' run, having received a pressing invitation from some friends to take a seat in their carriage. The day was bright and pleasant, and its rays were reflected from a thousand cheerful faces on the road—laughing and bantering as on they went—every care cast behind. Then the roadside inn, raised from its twelvemonth's stupour, and in astonishment at the sudden racket in its inside, looked joyous notwithstanding; while the "missis," and the daughter, and the young relation also had come to help, and the London waiter, hired for the occasion, looked as spruce and as fine as could be. We had first-rate cattle, and passed nearly everything. We reached the course early, and obtained a good position, close to the barrier and near the grand stand. Thousands upon thousands were there, out among the green hills, in God's country, bringing their seared and worldly hearts into the beautiful province of Nature. I lay back in the carriage and philosophised (it was after dinner and a glass of champagne), and I thought of Waterloo and the two great armies. The mass on the opposite hill, the cleared course between, and the solid masses of people on our side were soon transformed into the two contending armies; and I thought, *en passant*, how a little musket firing would soon bring me on to my legs on the other side of the vehicle. Instead of the popping of corks and the ring of laughter, the boom of artillery and the groans of the wounded would, I thought, alter the scene; and yet the light gallop of the noble horses, the gaily-clothed jockey, the swearing turf-man, the cunning thief, the clever conjuror, the blooming beauty, the fortune-teller and the fortune-hearer, the water-carrier, the beggar, the swell, the shoeblack, "three sticks a penny," and the policeman on duty, together with my lolling lazy self, would as effectually be carried away before sixty years hence as though the cannonade had been heavy, and the carnage dreadful, and the glory great

So up I got and saw the Derby run; and in the midst of the race I looked upon the mass of faces turned in eagerness on the struggling group of flying horses. In an instant the white faces all turned away, and black heads filled their places.

We had tea at the roadside inn as we returned; and the house appeared still more astonished, for the crowd had penetrated into the pretty back-garden where we had our tea. On the way home our good horses kept up their pace and we arrived in due time at our several destinations after a day of very delightful excitement.

15th June, 1853.—Yesterday up at 5.30, and to Willesden to see our station clear of some special trains of troops going to Staines by our South Western Junction. Then to Camden, to clear some troops brought from the steamer at Blackwall, by our Dock Junction, to Camden, for Weedon. To Haydon Square in the afternoon, then to Moggs, the map makers, and then back to work at Camden.

20th June, 1853.—Half an hour's chat with poor Mrs. Essen. She is very delicate, and frets still bitterly about her poor husband. These two folks, in one room, married some two or three years ago, but he failed to get work for nearly a twelvemonth, and they parted with all they had. At length he fortunately obtained employment on the railway, and they were *so* happy in their little home, gathering back their valuables, one by one; and when he was made brakesman, how they thanked God for their prosperity! for " he was a good young man and a kind husband," "always to his time," "smiling only if his dinner were not ready through some accident; " and she prided herself on never letting him come home to an unswept hearth. The last day he went away he said, "Good-bye, Eliza; " and a nervous feeling made her call him back to unsay the word, for it sounded unusual and strange. He smiled and said, "What shall I say?—Then farewell!" and so he went away, saying that he would be back to tea in good time. But the tea-time came without him, and hours passed away in awful doubt and fear, and then, weeping, she went as far as the railway gate, and saw some men in earnest talk with the gatekeeper, but she had no courage to ask for her husband. Home she went again; and when my messenger asked at the door for Mrs. Essen, she exclaimed, "Is my dear husband killed? Tell, oh, tell me, though it should kill me!" Then like the wind she flew to the hospital, to her dying partner on his last bed—he sensible and breathing her name; and when she saw that death was on him she bade him pray to God, and he replied, "Pray for me." Then the doctors forbade her to stay any longer, and sent her home, which was very hard for her to bear. With the dawn, after a sleepless night, she again entered the hospital, only to learn that her husband was gone, with his last accents naming his "dear wife."

22nd June, 1853.—I have just been superintending the turning in and unloading of the Leeds and Bradford goods; such a scuffle as it is!—men and horses, with scrambling, and hooting, and calling-over and scribbling, and everyone in his shirt-sleeves, and the horses perspiring. A few mornings ago a poor fellow was seen looking for the top of his finger, which lay on the buffer of a waggon. Terrible work! The age lives too fast. Nothing but top speed will satisfy the public. Every operation must be performed in keeping with the railway speed, and the government encouragement of competition in railways pushes the evil to a climax. The race into the City every morning between the Great Northern Company and us, with Leeds and Bradford packs, is dangerous in the extreme.

The railway to Fenchurch Street from here will run trains along our line, and the South Western junction out of it to Kew, Brentford, &c., on the 1st August next. Look at the map, and you will find that London will soon be "encompassed round about" with rails—from Fenchurch to Camden, Camden to Nine Elms, Nine Elms or thereabouts to the Crystal Palace (proposed).

I had a row with a cabman last week. He agreed to take my wife and me home from Tate's, and stopped short at the Gloucester Road; said his horse was restive, and wouldn't go in the dark. I got out, and wouldn't pay him. He followed all along the road with his cab, occasionally saying, "Ah! would you?" This was to his dunderhead horse, who enjoyed the quiet walk, and had no more thought of being restive, poor beast, than I have of becoming an opera-dancer. Then at my gate we had a shindy. He wanted to come in, and I shoved him out. I gave him a shilling, and he took it with threats of a summons next day if I didn't pay him more. I declined, and closed the gate. In a few minutes all was as still as death—the gas-lamp shone on the silent garden, the dog dosed, the white blinds drawn down told of stretched-out forms within, and the poor rats crept out of their holes to snatch the chickens' crumbs, the steady tread of the policeman died away in the distance, and the moon gazed down on all the town.

What do you think of our clergyman, Mr. G.? He has declined a living worth £1,000 per annum, because he thinks his work in this newly formed district is not finished. I rejoice to think that he stops with us. His stipend is £350.

23rd July, 1853.—A glance at G.'s conduct gives me a nudge, that other people too might be content without ambitious hankerings after Canada, &c.; that other people too have their work to complete amongst weak brothers and destitute sisters, and children worse than orphans; and that running away from it all may be deserting a sacred mission. Then ambition whispers that increased means give increased power to help—that money is better than sympathy—that, in rash attempts to rescue, the hero and sinking are often both lost. Well! *God help us all!* If patience and endurance could be struck out of the Christian's conditions, who would not wish to do some one great good in acknowledgment of his Maker's mercies—and die? Quitting the weary battle where the Devil charges at the head of his troops, now in the front and now in the rear, until the Christian's little column of good resolutions, at some fatal moment, fails to form the necessary square, and is crushed to the earth and annihilated.

26th July, 1853.—I had a call from an old acquaintance, A. R., who has a good business in the City. I learn a few things from him, such as manœuvres on 'Change, &c., which are amusing to hear about; but, knowing him to be rather loose in principle, I keep my hand on my sword all the time I am with him.

29th July, 1853.—Accidents on railways hunt in couples, or packs, as I have often told you. A few days ago an axle broke on the Trent Valley portion of our line. Last night a cattle train smashed into a goods train on the same line. The night before last a train of goods was shunted into this station before the proper signal was given, and sent a loaded truck and a horse attached to it topsy-turvy.

1st August, 1853.—I was very busy all day on Saturday selling salmon and meat and looking to the goods from a breakdown near Weedon on Friday night. An express train overtook a long goods' train and ran into it. The engine of the goods, 56 waggons' length off, was knocked off the line and the engine-driver sent head foremost into the coke; yet, strange to say, three drovers in the goods guard's van, the hindmost vehicle, asleep, escaped unhurt. The guard had not time to wake them. He jumped off into a ditch, and the drovers were found rolled up together like a ball of cotton. Nobody was injured except the express fireman, who had a nasty knock in the eye. The boxes of salmon, however, and the bales of goods flew about all over the premises. Three bullocks, also, turned a somersault out of a cattle waggon and for the moment felt a little surprise, but finding the grazing pretty good on the slope where they fell, they appeared to like the change and were discovered making the best of their opportunity.

* . * * * * *

Touching total abstinence from drink for example's sake. It would do good, doubtless, even one case would be a sufficient success. But the difficulties of such a resolution are very great. Many a friend, many an acquaintance, many a pleasant hour stolen from care by the exhilarating glass would be lost. The jocund laugh would be exchanged for the quiet smile ; and with the occasional morning's headache would go the evening's happy interchange of good fellowship. Men extract the happiness of many hours, and live it out in one, over the generous wine or the cheering grog. Virtue is its own reward ; health and a more general and thinly spread enjoyment is experienced by the abstinent man, and thrown into his bargain is an approving conscience, to light him heavenward. For my part, knocking about with railway people, I feel it would be next to impossible to turn my back upon the poison altogether. I have a serious desire, however, to keep it as far away as possible, considering the awful effect of its excessive use. It is certain that a moderate use of drink is a difficult and dangerous position to hold; like table-turning, one begins to move faster and faster until it becomes a labour to pull up.

9th August, 1853.—I have been up to my eyes in bother the last few days. One of my clerks had leave, and the clerk who did his duty fell sick, and a third placed to the work got drunk. Then I had much trouble in disposing of the corpse of a titled lady sent to us by the South Western Company for Carlisle. Then two waggons were upset on the line, and a sudden increase of business crammed up the station, and the new Kew trains stopped and hindered our work, and the engine turntable broke and caused all the passenger engines to cross our lines, and waggons and tarpaulins grew scarce, and I ate some cucumber and made myself ill, and some boys attempted to get over our garden wall and steal our apples, and some beef I bought went bad, and my potatoes took the disease, and a schoolfellow bothered me for a berth, and a new boot gave me a corn, and bread rose to $8\frac{1}{2}$d. per loaf, and the butcher's book struck me all of a heap, and another smash occurred to a goods train at Roade.

11th August, 1853.—Thieves are pilfering the goods from our waggons here to an impudent extent. We are at our wits' end to find out the blackguards. Not a night passes without wine hampers, silk parcels, drapers' boxes, or provisions being robbed; and if the articles are not valuable enough they leave them about the station. A roll of chintz was found on the station this morning; of course mistaken at first sight for silk, but on tearing the paper the plunderer discovered it to be chintz and threw it away in disgust. I wish he would send in his claim for his loss of time. He should be paid in full.

12th August, 1853.—In yesterday's *Times* you will see the continuation of a paper about a French Commission on War. I have not read the preceding article, but in this it is amusing to read how neatly the Gallic cock disposes of us poor English. He talks of cooking our goose with the utmost ease; but Monsieur will have to get another pair of breeches before he takes the wind out of our little men who "go down to the sea in ships," and after he has licked them and got on shore he won't find it quite such pleasant walking as in the gardens of the Tuilleries. We should manage to keep him on the alert. Then you would see young Stevenson at the head of his Camden Station Irregulars, slaughtering the enemy and bathed in their blood; and when the fight was done behold him decorated with the Garter and elevated to a dukedom, say of Montrose, &c., &c.

17th August, 1853.—A friend has just asked my opinion on a private matter. I believe we all consult our own inclinations and decide in the main, in most cases, before we appeal to the wisdom of our friends. How high our estimation of their judgment if they approve! how deep our suspicion of their motives if they condemn!

18th August, 1853.—I am continually bothered with my men. Some resign to emigrate, some get drunk and are discharged, and others are hurt. There is a difficulty in obtaining strong fellows who read and write, and can lead a horse for our night and day work. The sturdy fellows, too, are as independent as possible. Work is plentiful, and the new land of promise so desirable a resource, that we have to pet our good hands. By-and-by, I shall have to lift my hat and say, "Oh, Mister John Porter, will you do me the favour to turn that waggon? Thank you. Pray take care of yourself there; and, John Porter, sir, would you like to take Mrs. J. P. and the family down the line on Sunday? I shall be happy to pass you. And, John, if there should be anything nice in the train, amongst the goods, which you would like to have, pray help yourself. I wish you to feel quite comfortable and unrestrained." It is fast coming to this; and if John Porter gets drunk, instead of dismissing the honest fellow, I shall have to say, "Why, John, my boy, you've had a little beer! Allow me to fetch a cab, and if you feel ill to-morrow, you need not hurry in the morning."

19th August, 1853.—I had a long argument last night with Mr. R., a pale-faced vegetarian. I have seldom met with so clear-headed and clever a man. Politics, natural philosophy, finance, medicine,—he is fluent in all; and his opinions on most subjects comprehend the bearings of the matter in such a grasp that his judgment seems unerring. Such is the perspicuity of his remarks and reasoning, that one is inclined to confidence in his conclusions. He announced his disbelief in the existence of the Devil, in eternal punishment, in Christ's actually fasting forty days, in the Devil's placing Christ on a pinnacle of the temple, or an exceeding high mountain, to behold all the kingdoms of the world. He treated the whole as figurative; Eve's temptation by a serpent, as it is narrated, he laughed at as an absurd fable, taken literally. Tell me this: is it anywhere commented upon as to the manner in which it became known to the evangelists that Christ so fasted, and was tempted? I shall be glad if you can give me a reference to any book which meets liberally and fairly the objections of this sort, which will arise in one's mind, notwithstanding that the regular orthodox churchman will not condescend to notice their existence.

22nd August, 1853.—I reached Weedon about six o'clock on Saturday evening, and proceeded with Charlie and two of his friends in a dog-cart, thirty-five miles across country to Stratford-on-Avon. The ride was delightful. We baited twice on the journey, and as we rode through Leamington and Warwick, I recognised the places where, seven years ago, my wife and I strolled in the enjoyment of our honeymoon. By ten o'clock we had our legs under the supper-table of Charlie's friend, Mr. Hartley, proprietor of the Golden Lion hotel. Mine host is a jolly fellow, a good singer, and has such floods of anecdotes, told with all the manner and wit of an accomplished actor. Hartley is a celebrated comedian for a hundred miles round, and might have an engagement in London immediately, if he chose, but he finds the Golden Lion suits him better. He is one of five sons of a schoolmaster, who died when they were all young, except the eldest, and he only eighteen years of age. This young man kept on the school, and brought up the family. All the brothers dined with us yesterday, and a good dinner and a good bottle of wine we had—and roars of laughter. In the morning we visited the church, saw the tomb of the bard, and went thence to the house where Ann Hathaway, Shakespeare's wife, resided. A descendant of the Hathaway's showed me an old bedstead, and the kitchen where Will did his courting. We started at seven, and drove back to Weedon. A pipe, and a chat with Charlie's wife, and then to bed; not, however, before Charlie and I had rushed out with the poker to some imaginary thieves, who turned out to be the dog pitching into a birch-broom, and nearly choking himself. A train brought me home this morning by eleven o'clock, to hosts of papers, and the usual shindy.

* * * * * * *

> The lines proceed, the pages fill—
> And tell the hues of life's swift thread;
> Soon will it cease, the pen be still,
> The hand that guides it, cold and dead.

1st September, 1853.—You and I, in common with all other men of fixed income, will be the sufferers if corn becomes scarce and provisions rise still higher than their present disagreeable rate. Thank God, the prospect of a war is more remote than it was; but the singular blights now apparent in potatoes, grapes, and other products, the strange weather of the last eight months, and the introduction of so much gold, together with the emigration of our miners and sailors, and other men of thews and sinews, all proclaim that an extraordinary epoch is coming. The mighty billows of Time are rolling on, in the palm of the Wonderful Creator. We tiny, but not unnoticed or forgotten mites, in the boundless scheme, may go on with our work—I to my merchandise and you to your souls—always remembering, amid discouragement and difficulty, that "He that goeth forth and weepeth, bearing precious seed, shall doubtless come again with rejoicing, bringing his sheaves with him."

21st September, 1853.—At a trial at Westminster. It would make your heart bleed to see some of the wretched criminals and their heart-broken friends. I saw several respectable-looking young men, from eighteen to [illegible] age, well-dressed and intelligent, tried [illegible] &c. Some overwhelmed with [illegible]; others scowling at [illegible] clever young men [illegible] talent, but who [illegible] embezzlement [illegible] to cure all [illegible] render the judge and the advocate, the detective, the gaoler, and the criminal, things of the past ; to banish temptation and take away the staircase of error and sin by which men descend, step by step, to perdition! Simply let us say, "Thy Kingdom come!"

28th September, 1853.—My solemn oration on the decease of Mr. Samuel Warren would probably amuse that gentleman. All you say of the two authors, now that you mention it, comes up in my memory as something I knew well before but had forgotten. I have read the "Diary of the Late Physician," and "Ten Thousand a Year," and have heard of the other man's "Crescent and the Cross," and cannot think how I could confuse the two persons. But what have I to do with your novels and polite literature? Don't I live in a real, tragic, comic, stirring drama— more strange than any fiction; Don't my heroes and heroines keep me wide awake? Is there not an absorbing act continually on the stage,—parcels, porters, and the public, horses, carts, correspondence, careless clerks, and curious coincidences, &c.,&c.? What, then, have I to do with your literature? Pshaw, Sir! I am one of your philosophers, who distil their own ingredients to manufacture the elixir of life, and don't buy them at the apothecary's. I take my stones from the quarry, not from the picturesque ruins of another man's building. At least, this is a good excuse for my ignorance of the *belles lettres*. Am I not a mysterious work myself? Have I yet read myself? Have I sufficiently studied that portion of the book which will live for ever? Can I reflect on the pages of my existence which I have scampered through, without a painful and absorbing interest? And when the time comes for me to return the book to the Giver, shall I not with shame review the thumbed and soiled leaves, and deserve a terrible award for my unprofitable use of it?

4th October, 1853.—The swelling river shines solemnly in the sunlight, and on its trusty bosom, the mariner cunningly shifts the sails of his craft, using the fickle wind to take his treasure far up the stream to the busy port; while he, and the many mighty ships which join him on the way, bearing the varied produce of the world, meet the many others outward bound, and make a busy scene. Ride we in the eager steamboat, full of tired human beings fleeing from their toil. The thread-bare tunes from harp and violin engage the crowd, while such as you and I lean over the bulwarks, and gaze on the surrounding spectacle. When first I looked on yonder shore, taken to Gravesend on a cockney jaunt, I was a wan, and spare, and tiny boy, and that great house was building for one, 'twas said, who had been a lawyer and had defended thieves, and,.having gained great civic honours, and a princely fortune, was rearing that great dwelling there, to end his days in. Since that time, my friend, what deaths I have seen—what poverty, what sickness, what changes in circumstance and feeling—what friendships I have formed, what love requited, what errors committed! Now just heaves in view a pretty hamlet. The church and red-roofed houses, quay and pier and mill, look cheerful, nestling beneath chalk cliffs and verdant hills, with dotted woodlands here and there. Surely peace and industry must here combine, and happiness and Christian charity; no scandal, no tyranny, no vice of any kind! Prithee, step on shore and see.

* * o * * *

Oh! my Turnbull, come back to Whitchurch, where at least *some* virtue may be found!

7th October, 1853.—The ball-room at Chalk Farm Tavern is no more. It has been taken down to make way for some new houses. And, so, farewell, thou scene of gents and dirty muslin! At one time, I suppose, greater swells frequented the place—white kids, cravats, and well-cut coats, and fair forms charmingly arrayed; but they all went their way, and of late years "sixpenny hops" have made night hideous there,—soldiers and servant maids, dirty drabs, and dangerous "young fellers" in curious clothing, with short pipes and wonderfully unclean hands,—such a set! and they, too, are all gone!

9th October, 1853.—At Euston Station last night the engine ran against a signalman, and, catching him in the back and neatly lodging his hat on the buffer-beam, sent him flying. He fell not on the rails, but between them, and escaped with whole bones. Now, that is what I call a close shave. These things make one nervous for a day or two. A sharp shunt or a shout, and the swish of the engine, when one is between our numerous lines, makes the heart leap into the mouth and the lips hold tight, particularly at night.

13th October, 1853.—What a pucker the local authorities are all in about the cholera! I see one placard, amongst other things, recommends the people of London never to drink any but pure water. That is waggish, and we shouldn't joke when the cholera is coming.

I am taking an hour's ride on horseback again every day when the weather permits. The woods and trees around Hampstead are donning the russet suit again.

> Again untiring Autumn brings the golden leaves,
> And clothes the trees in beauty ere it leaves them bare;
> So He who shed His blood between the thieves
> Was first with grandeur decked in robe of purple rare.
> But, as He rose,—though leafless boughs too soon they'll be,
> Left to the sport and scorn of every passing wind,
> A drear and bitter season over, they will see
> Return of hopeful life to cheer and bless mankind.

18th October, 1853.—I paid a visit yesterday afternoon to the Hanwell Lunatic Asylum. As soon as we had passed the door and stood on the well staircase of the interior, amid many iron bars, made as cheerful as possible with light blue paint, I felt we were inside a madhouse. Squatted in unlikely places and in uncomfortable and unexpected attitudes, poor demented women met the view, staring, simpering, smiling, giggling, declaiming, or swearing; and others, equally sad to see, absorbed in silent madness. In the refractory wards higher up—for the large well staircase has several landings, with wards opening upon each—there were creatures in petticoats, with stubbly hair and distorted ill-shapen faces, lounging about and raving and blaspheming if spoken to. Others made absurd noises; others twiddled their fingers as though playing the flute. One poor wretch was gobbling exactly like a turkey, and another informed me that she (the gobbler) was "always at it,"—"it was strange, but do what she would with her, she would make that noise,"—"now, for her part, her uncle's name was Herring, and her own name was Thatcher." Poor Thatcher! They said she was a hard-working well-disposed patient. A lady in checked clothing offered me some bread, and another asked me if I was for England and Victory; while a third woke up from a deep reverie, as she sat, tailor-fashion, on her bed, and cursed me lustily. One demanded whom I had come to see, and then consigned me to perdition. An old woman—I noticed that most of the women were old—was performing some tragic and by no means ungraceful gestures, with denunciation of an awful kind against some person best known to herself. She was, however, locked up before she had concluded, and there her tongue *was* let loose. The young woman who was her keeper said, "She never strikes. All noise." In a small ward an old respectable-looking lady said that her heart was broken and had been so a long, long time; and in the next breath, in reply to a contradiction, she exclaimed, "No, certainly not; if my heart were broken I shouldn't be here." When reminded that she had just stated before that her heart *was* broken, she replied, "Ah, I *said* so. I say a many things!" I think there are many people at large as insane as this respectable old woman. I found one wild-looking female standing behind me with a handful of knives, which rather surprised me, to say the least of it; but, on examination, the implements proved to be harmless, only about an inch or so of the blade being at all sharp, and the remainder the sixteenth of an inch in thickness. I enquired if the mad folks knew that these were different from ordinary knives. The keeper smiled and replied, "Quite well. In fact, they know almost everything, even to the shame of being in a madhouse." A very mad lady-like woman, with remains of much beauty, said, in answer to the keeper, that she was much better, as must be clear to her, for otherwise she would have been unable to move. This patient was said to be highly accomplished. In the matron's dining-room we found a nice-looking old person. On seeing me look at the portrait of Dr. Connolly, which hung in the room, she broke out into fervent admiration of the man. "Ah, sir! every insane person should pray for that good man. I have been here fifteen years and can remember the time when an iron belt and chain fastened us to the wall and we were treated cruelly. Many, many years was that good gentleman trying to get the system altered, and he succeeded at last." The keeper told us that this was all true, but that the old person who had addressed us had been getting rather worse in her malady lately. All praise to the good and great man who created such a feeling of gratitude in a madwoman's heart! A look into another ward, where a 'Queen' sitting in state at one end of the table, and an old wretch, who cursed the keeper for asking for her beer, at the other; and this finished the female side.

The men were more orderly. They were sitting about on seats, some reading, others smoking. One crept behind my friend and tried to pinch his leg, but this was in a refractory ward, and was the only instance of the kind we saw. The men looked worst in the epileptic ward, bloated, spooney, heavy. The other wards contained some fine, handsome young men, with high foreheads. Many of them touched their hats and rose as we passed. One man told me that he and his brothers had had some money left them, and that it worried him and they sent him there; "now, wasn't that a hard case?" Another—a fine old man-of-war's man—gave me an account of their having taken away his pension and shoved him in there; and another interrupted him with the consoling remark that it was "only for life, Bill." The men bake, brew, make all the clothes and shoes and bedding, print, and perform, in short, all the labour of the building.

Are you tired of this long rigmarole about insanity? Well, what is your opinion on the subject? I am inclined to believe the theory of the man who made out that we were all mad. The madhouses only contain the worst cases. Most of the people at Hanwell seem to have the string of their ideas cut, and all their thoughts kicking about in their brains anyhow. There are few of us, I fear, who have the string very loose sometimes, and the notions get into the most improper places in our noddles occasionally. We sane folks who pity our poor mad brethren so complacently! In the Asylum one lunatic laughs at his companion's delusion, but goes stark with his own. What are we doing out of the Asylum—in the pulpit, on the platform, in the press? Why, laughing at each other's delusions and going into our own "like mad." What is more insane than the propensity to do just what we know to be evil, in spite of the warnings of conscience, and to incur Divine vengeance for the sake of a few years of feverish neglect of God's commands?

24th September, 1853.—All the past week our station has been in a mess. Goods accumulating, agents neglectful, reports, denials, proofs, waggons off the line, pilferages, indignant public, wonderful influx of potatoes from the north, remonstrance with general manager on the filthy state of the station, brakesmen crushed between the buffers, alteration of trains, new regulation to put detonating fog-signals several hundred yards in the rear of any train coming to a stand on the line, in addition to using the hand signal (this in consequence of the Irish accident), sickness amongst the porters, sickness amongst the horses.

25th October, 1853.—In the extreme state of insanity, women are the more noisy and gesticulatory of the two sexes; and the peculiarity ascends the scale. The most sensible woman is a greater scold than her parallel companion, the most sensible man. When a man is talkative and violent in his remonstrances, appears to me a mark of effeminacy. The calm and dignified manner, the few pointed words of biting reproof, or earnest exhortation, are the attributes of a *man*.

27th October, 1853.—Some of the clerks here are getting up a Mutual Instruction and Discussion Society. We have a small Reading Room in Pickford & Co.'s department, and I met the clerks last night and read to them a little paper as a sort of inaugural address. In it I contrasted the present aspect of our station and its surroundings with the green fields and lanes which formerly occupied the site—the peaceful rural scene where the modest daisy raised its face to the sun, the violet shed its perfume, and the lark ascended with its morning song to heaven. I showed how much we were indebted to the labours of our ancestors, and spoke of the duty attaching to each one of us to cultivate our own minds, and thereby, in a humble way, to help forward the general progress of our country and of the human race.

4th November, 1853.—I was in the City yesterday and this morning. As a novelty there is much to contemplate in the commencement of a City morning. About 7 or 8 a.m. the outskirts of the great hive of the insect called Man is all alive in the upper rooms, with the said insect in his shirt sleeves, applying a bright sharp instrument to his chin. Then thousands of them descend the stairs, rave about, put on boots, eat and drink something, and sally forth. Then a race commences towards the centre of the Hive; and away they pour, some riding, some on foot,—thicker and closer; mingling, at length, with the dirty dwellers in that place towards which they are rushing. As they thicken, and drop off at the little cells where they stop all day, you may see their faces grow more grave; and although in the throng you might take them to be all of one species, an inspection of a few of the cells would show you that there are many degrees among them. See the " great " man in that inner cell lecturing the younger insect on the evils of dissipation. Well,—they were *both* drunk last night,—one at his own table with wine, the other at a tavern, on gin and water. See that stout old insect crawling into yonder cell. He meets one of the dirty dwellers,—a female of the species. He tells her that times are hard and prices low, and that he can't give her more than sixpence per dozen for shirts.

But there are the good cells, where excellent things are done all day long, by rich but hard-working men, who keep up the gradual improvement of the great hive. What a morning's walk we could take together, meditating on these things.

23rd November, 1853.—You will smile when I tell you that I am on the paper in the Reading-room of our little Society for " A few remarks on Geology." Of course! What do you mean by jeering? Didn't I study under Professor Sedgwick at the University of Cambridge? Didn't I listen to that learned man for a whole hour one wet day? What do you say? A mere compilation? Well, suppose it be, as far as technicalities go; is there anything new under the sun? At any rate the reflections and remarks will be my own, and that is all that I announce. Be off, Bob; don't bully me.

27th April, 1854.—The day's work is over. The papers are cleared away or stowed under weights, to rest during the darkness. The clerks are gone, the office sounds hollow, and the calm evening invites me to take my departure. I hasten away. The pause on this restless place will be brief. The night clerks, porters, horses, and engines will soon be here, to pull and haul and shriek and shout and hurry and drive.

30*th April*, 1854.—In some moments a blessed hope illumines my mind, and I believe confidently that, when this world of sin and sorrow and disappointment shall close on my view for ever, a sweet voice of forgiveness and mercy will ring joyfully in my ear; that Jesus Christ will wash my polluted soul from sin; that that wonderful sacrifice—that almost incredible system of unbounded love will be realised by me. Hasten, O happy hour! Who could not long that the shadows might thicken for a moment, to be dispelled for ever? Who would not be eager to exchange this world, how blessed soever it may be, for that glorious land, the splendour of which eye hath not seen and the heart of man cannot conceive? Think of purity and glory and brightness and love, unalloyed and unfading for ever.

4*th May*, 1854.—Last night I dined at the Hanover Square Rooms with no end of parsons. One of the cloth got very 'tight.' He d—d everybody and nearly punched my head. He's repenting at his leisure this morning, I reckon. The Bishop of Chester made a good speech—a little too long perhaps. The dinner was not the best I ever sat down to, and there was great uproar in getting the hats and coats, coming out. The parsons, who are no doubt nearly all unseasoned casks, were very boisterous.

16*th May*, 1854.—George Campbell felt his feet very cold the other night, and said so, and got up and wrapped himself in warmer clothes; but the fire was flickering within, though he knew it not, and the poor old man died while dressing himself in the morning. He was a random talking old fellow, and irreligious apparently; but who knows how far he outraged his conscience, under the impression that it was necessary to suit his conversation to his hearers, whom he thought irreligious? Who shall say what passed between himself and God, in the quiet hour when the world was shut out and conscious guilt and fear accused him on his knees?

5*th June*, 1854.—What a long correspondence I have had with the Countess of ———— about the threepences charged for her empty baskets! I had a few notes last year, but this year she has gone on anyhow. There's more bother about a nobleman's vegetables, or a parson's wife's new cap, sent by luggage train than about all the provisions for the fleet or ten thousand bales for China. You aristocrats ought to send by passenger train only. Why, your butler or your cook prigs more in a week than would pay for the vegetable basket or the hamper of foul linen for twelve months. And yet the portly Samuel and Mrs. Dripping escape, while we Railway innocents are called extortionists, and cheats, and monopolists, and get abused in the most fearful terms, but generally in pure grammar.

28th June, 1854.—Bells in steeples don't like playing tunes. They do it evidently under protest,—especially the sacred tunes. There are our Hampstead bells, now. They struggle through the familiar psalm-tunes in a most agonising manner. The quick notes are not at all solemn; they have a 'nix my dolly, pals' inclination which outrages one's sense of propriety. Since the man greased one of the slowest sacred airs, the other day, and it darted off, to his horror, at polka pace, the notes have settled down into respectable time; but the clergyman had better have left the steeple to play "Peas and Beans," as it used to do until he was scandalised by the secular sounds; for the alteration to sacred tunes exclusively is a dead failure.

6th July, 1854.—I am very much down in the dumps. I find myself inclined to grumble at everyone, and when anything turns up that gives me a reasonable opportunity to grumble with a fair cause, why, I go in and win. Win, did I say? No, I don't win much; I leave off worse tempered than before. I have heard of a sea-captain who used to retire occasionally and have half-an-hour's hard swearing by himself, in which he is said to have found great relief. I haven't tried this.

11th July, 1854.—On Sunday I dined with a friend at Watford and enjoyed a delightful walk to Stanmore and Bushey Heath. My friend's aunt, an old lady, lives in a picturesque cottage near his house, and the indentical 'Mr. Dick' lives with her. He is an old chap now,—off his head, as our nurse calls it. He dosen't chink his money, as Dickens tells; but if they give him any he throws it away *instanter*. He likes to be talked to, and listens to conversation, and makes comical noises when he laughs; but he seldom says anything except 'yes' or 'no.' He is rich, and his brother, who is also his heir, thinks he will soon die, but

Mr. Dick seems inclined to hang on sturdily. Now, whether Dickens ever stumbled across this 'Mr. Dick' or not, I cannot tell; but his name is Dick, and the similarity of the characters in name and intellect and other things is singular.

Last night, after I was used-up at the station, I strolled to Hampstead. There were the omnibuses, and the rough fellows at the end of Flask Walk, and the Station-house, and Hankin's, and George Kerrison, who looks older, talking to Cornick, the man who has Watson's shop; and there was Livock's Alley; and there the place where the garden used to be,—for they have built a house in it, which you will be surprised to learn. The poor new house appears to feel its false position; the whole thing looks uncomfortable. The calm evening resting tranquilly on the fresh green undulating landscape, the stillness heightened by the cowboys' call to the cattle, and the gratification which one always feels at gazing upon a wide expanse far out, had a sweet effect on my mind; and the railway clerk forgot, for the moment, his station, and thought pure thoughts full of aspiration, beyond the toil and struggle of the city at his back, and, —— but the fever I lately had has made me spooney, I think, at times.

18*th July*, 1854.—My wife and I, and three of the bairns, are staying at Hemel Hempstead, near Boxmoor station. The ride to and from Camden daily is doing me good. There are beautiful walks in the neighbourhood of the town, and we shall all benefit by the change. Hemel Hempstead is a quiet place, with about 8,000 inhabitants, who retire to bed at 10 p.m. They have public-houses, but the publicans go to church like christians, and nobody appears to get drunk. The church is a Norman edifice, with a fine spire. Inside there is a hideous gallery, and the organ is a bad one; but there are two good stained-glass windows. When the creed is said, people and priest turn to the communion table—which ought to be announced beforehand to strangers seated in the chancel, as they suddenly find themselves turned round upon by the whole congregation, which is embarrassing. There is an absurd old countryman, with a queer-shaped head, and a dissipated-looking white choker, who *will* stare about the church, and who holds in his hand a stick with a sort of cruet on the top of it. Apart from these eccentricities, the church on Sunday is a pleasing sight. How many years the sun has shone through those old windows on the same scene, though the actors have been replaced over and over again! What a serious moral those venerable walls seem to preach!

20th July, 1854.—The Hemel Hempstead straw-plaiters are to be met with all over the town. They talk, and walk, and look about, and loiter, and listen, while their fingers all the time spin away at the straw, turning it into plaits fit for sewing into bonnets. Women, old and young, lovers and wives, and little children, are all engaged in this manufacture, and you find them at work in all sorts of places—at the cottage doors, at the corners of streets, in Sir Astley Cooper's beautiful park, by the stream, in the fields, and by the fire-side. It is said that the young women grow up to be bad wives, and that the little children make dirty plait, which fetches a low price.

There is a service at the church here every day, but I am told that the clergyman's wife is very often the only person present besides his Reverence.

Have you read Mrs. Crowe's "Night-side of Nature?"—such a book about ghosts! Take care that you do not see my double walk into your premises some of these days. Certain it is that if the spirit lingers near those whom the heart has esteemed, mine is very likely to pay you a visit ere it wings its flight. Well, it isn't pleasant to meet the ghost of the dearest friend if one steps into the garden after dusk; so, we'll drop the subject, and hope that nothing of the kind will happen.

4th August, 1854.—Yesterday my friend, Mr. Taylor, of the Steam Flour Mill adjoining Camden Station, took me to his house in the country to dinner. I popped away at three o'clock, and we reached Rickmansworth, four miles from Watford station, about 4.30. I was driven up a beautiful avenue of trees, into a square space, bounded on two sides by an Elizabethan mansion, and on the other two by trees and a stream of water, across which there is a pretty view of the church and a wood. Surprised—for I had expected to find quite a different kind of dwelling—I walked through the spacious oaken hall and into the panelled dining-room, and then into the drawing-room, and shook hands with the miller's two young daughters and their governess.

Dinner wouldn't be ready for an hour or more, so I consented to my friend's proposal to take a turn in the grounds, glad of the opportunity of examining the fine old place. It had been for centuries the manor-house of a family of the name of Whitfield, who gradually sold their land and died out, leaving the house and some acres around in Chancery. My friend bought the house, and twenty-five or thirty acres, and had the misfortune to lose his wife just as he was about to remove to the beautiful place. He occupies about half the house; the remaining rooms are empty and silent—the very air of them seems mournful Wide staircases, sprawling hinges, stained-glass windows, oak carving, gables outside and mysterious passages within, contrast strangely with the homely habits of the occupants—yet I question much if the shining panels of the large dining-room ever looked down upon a better scene than that in which the honest old gentleman took the principal part, when he read aloud a chapter from the Bible to his daughters, their governess, and myself. His sonorous voice gave forth the Holy Words with an impressive emphasis, befitting his venerable appearance. During the prayer which followed, a stranger, gazing through the window from without, might have supposed the miller, with his grey hair and white neckcloth, to be the family chaplain; while the kneeling forms of the daughters and their governess, with those of your David and the two servants, filled up a consistent background. I slept in an immense room. The great bed of Ware could not have been larger than the enormous concern towards which I journeyed after putting out the light on the huge dressing-table. I slept soundly. Whether the restless spirits of any of the Whitfield family hovered about the room I know not. The witching hours passed over, and I awoke when the bell rang. I had a brisk walk to my clothes on the chair, and thence to the washstand, which gave me an appetite for my breakfast.

15th August, 1854.—The strike of the drivers has harassed us immensely this week. It is a mistake, however, to suppose that they are skilled mechanics. When railways first commenced skilled mechanics drove the engines, but they gradually left the employment, and now a cleaner becomes a fireman and then a driver. A few months' experience gives them the requisite knowledge, which is much more simple than people suppose.

A terrible accident occurred last night on our Fenchurch Street Branch. The last train of goods from Haydon Square came to a stand for want of water, on an inclined plane at Highbury. The engines ran away for a supply, the men in charge thinking that the waggons would remain stationary. Unfortunately, however, the waggons ran back and met an advancing passenger train full tilt. The driver of the passenger train was killed on the spot. The fireman is not expected to recover, and one of my number-takers has also little chance of recovery. Four or five men in the break-van of the goods train escaped by a jump at the last moment, and the van was knocked into a complete smash—to use a moderate expression. Yet, with all this, the passengers escaped with a few bruises—an extraordinary result.

19th August, 1854.—Years ago I climbed the coke-oven chimney shaft here. It was newly built, and was esteemed a wonder. Three towering shafts marked Camden Station, from whatever point round London one viewed the prospect. Two of these long since sank into a heap of bricks. This week the last of our landmarks was hauled down, and a few minutes and a "hurrah!" restored the column of air it had so long displaced.

20th August, 1854.—Well, here I sit in tranquility, after a week of more than usual bustle and excitement. The events which have occurred, death from disease and accident, and change of all kinds, bring my thoughts at this moment to the text of Scripture "My times are in Thy hand." How terrible, yet how consoling, is this truth! How universal, yet how individually applicable! The nations of the earth may cry peace, and in the pride of a vaunted civilisation, say, "Behold our mighty progress, the work of our hands!"—but God, in whose hand their times are, may prove there is no peace. National sin is visited, and the great design of the Creator is carried forward. The pursuit of medical science may be so successfully prosecuted that mankind becomes almost exempt from violent suffering, when, behold, a scourge appears, to baffle all remedy and puzzle the most skilful and profound efforts of human aid,—bringing the boasting creature to confess that his times are in the hands of his Creator. Send forth the reapers, O, favoured

England, into thy overladen fields, swelling with their luxuriant crops of golden food; humbly thrust in the sickle and with grateful heart gather into thy garners the blessed harvest; and, while the manly voices of the toiling sons rend the air with rejoicing that the last load is secured, let thy swelling heart confess that lightning and tempest, and rot and blight, might have snatched the yellow prize from thy eager hand, that cholera might have left thee without labour to collect the store before the storms of winter consigned it to destruction. Boast not thyself, for thy times are in God's hand. Thou sowest, God has given thee the increase. Eat thou the bread of thankfulness, for the tramp of armed enemies is far removed from thy peaceful fields; thy comfortable firesides know not the ruthless intrusion of the desolating soldier; oh, boast not thyself, for the battle is not *always* to the strong. Long may the glorious season of harvest-time yield thee the fulness of the earth! Long may the beauty of thy landscapes be heightened by the glorious clothing, over hill and dale, of rich verdure and waving corn! Long may thy wonderful fleets be spared the storm, and experience that immunity from defeat which has so singularly attended them, to protect thy shores from each hostile attack! But remember in thy day of prosperity that the earth is the Lord's and the fulness thereof. To the gay, to the grave, the prosperous and the unfortunate, to the hoping and the successful, and the bereaved, and the broken-hearted, this text, like many others in the Blessed Book, applies alike with great force. A merciful Providence veils the future from our eyes, and coming events seldom cast their shadows before. Otherwise the gloom of a future reverse would embitter a long period of previous existence. God has commanded us what to do and be saved, and bids us cast our care upon Him. If we suffer, we may feel assured that it is to some wise end. Cheerful resignation will be blessed by increased fortitude to bear our burden, and teach us to say with humility, "My times are in Thy hand." Let not, however, the reckless and defiant sceptic think to escape the confession. The time will come; even his next movement may wring it from him. He may step into the next railway train smiling, confident—and a few minutes may see him in the *débris* of a collision, mangled and helpless. The morning may smile on his buoyant step, and the night may fling its pall over him, stark and dead in the silent room. He may form his plans for the progress and eminence of his darling offspring, but their times are in God's hands, and he may unexpectedly have to don the sombre garments of mourning for their early death, and lay down his schemes and the pride and hope of his heart—that heart which God, in His mercy, by such visitations converts to Himself. By these and many other means God often obliges the worldly, self-relying man to confess His holy name; but "blessed are they that have not seen and yet have believed." Blessed, indeed, is the man who has learnt early to rely on his Maker. The storms of affliction may burst over him, sorrow and poverty may overtake him; but he has a Friend who can and will guide and comfort him in all seasons. His house is built upon a rock.

"Praise the Lord, O my soul, and all that is within me praise His holy name.
Praise the Lord, O my soul, and forget not all His benefits;
Who forgiveth all thy sins and healeth all thine infirmities;
Who saveth thy life from destruction and crowneth thee with mercy and loving-kindness;
Who satisfieth thy mouth with good things and maketh thee young and lusty as an eagle."

30*th August*, 1854.—
On an engine, in the night-time,
  Flying through the starlit gloom;
Not a word between us spoken:
  On great caution hangs our doom.
Watch the gauge—turn on the water—
  Ope the gleaming furnace-door,
Making us appear like demons,
  In the glare, and smoke, and roar!
Ho! the signal! Put the break on!
  Shut off steam—reverse the gear!
Now the monster throbs and struggles,
  While we stare ahead and fear.
To man's frail limbs the mighty engine
  Yields obedience, and we stand
Beneath the lofty danger-signal.
  (Isn't this description grand?)

11*th September*, 1854.—More than usual to-day. I came to the office fresh and vigorous for work, and a more than usual amount of vexation, hurry, and irregularity has taken the shine out of me. Now I'm going home jaded and inclined to be ill-tempered. So on and on and on. When will it end? It's a horse-mill sort of business, this life of ours. Sleep and dream and eat and work, and sleep again. True, while we go round, the devil or man throws a brick at us, or lashes us, or breaks our shins, and so stirs us up; and then again we are turned out into the green fields for a day occasionally. But for the most part it is grind, grind.

> "Around, around, around,
> About and still about;
> All ill come running in,
> All good keep out."

13th September, 1854.—Poor George Watson died on Sunday night last, about 10 p.m. He had been ill for four or five weeks with a diseased heart, from which he was not expected to recover; but a two days' attack of diarrhœa hastened the crisis.

Taking a glance at George's career as a specimen of human life, what a troubled streak of existence it appears! An indulged boyhood—moral and practical struggling in manhood, in which poor George continually had the worst of it—and an early grave. The book is filled, and its pages are waste paper. How contemptible our fuming and puffing, our important anxieties and hopes, our scheming and grasping appear, when brought to this test! But that we are assured that the all-wise Creator fulfils some design in giving us this cunningly devised frame and these few years of life, we could not but turn away from the consideration of our pilgrimage as a worthless puzzle. I do not make these reflections in a gloomy spirit. Such thoughts kick off the ambition, self-importance, and anxious care from a man's heart, and allow simpler and purer pursuits to occupy him. He gives vent to love and kindness, stoops closer to the domestic affections, doffs his dignity, smiles at insults, has a hand and a cheering word for his erring and fallen brother, and a gentle feeling to all around him, knowing, as he does, that it is all gliding away—swiftly, surely, gliding away. The white hair in his head neither shames nor startles him; it is all in keeping with what his heart daily tells him. He pities and encourages, and goes about humbled and hopeful, waiting for the end. Such, it strikes me, must be the result to a man whose mind habituates itself to such musings, and is not tossed and driven by every wind of excitement and temptation.

18th September, 1854.—Nine horses lame and sick. Enough to grizzle one to fiddle-strings ! It is a good thing they're not my own property. I should wish the cat had me.

To the junction, five miles down, at 6 p.m. Back into the City by 8. To a Manchester agent at 9.30, and home at midnight.

25th September, 1854.—What can be said of the war ?—of the mangling and smashing and ruining of peaceable people, of the mock glory, of the train of desolated widows and orphans, of the hardened men who come away from the bloody work to dwell amongst us again ? There they go, bold hearts who deny that they see fear—keeping down, down, the inward quake about the soul, bright in colouring and gold and steel, beneath their flags. Yonder the host proceeds. Soon will the still small voice be drowned in excitement; soon death, sudden stone-dead death, miserable, agonising, frenzied death, and death under the surgeon's knife! And medals will be struck, and the band will play, and the Bishops will thank God, and subscriptions will pour in to try to fill the crevices in the rent hearts of the *poor* mothers and wives, and the *rich* mothers and wives must go up-stairs and weep, and time will cement over the disfigured parts of the social fabric ; and there an end of the success against the Russians.

Can it be that Napoleon, whose best means of securing his position on the throne is a firm alliance with respectable England,—can it be that he, not a young man, has deep schemes of revenging Waterloo? I can scarcely believe it. I think he likes enjoyment. Will he not prefer to grasp it for the rest of his life, rather than endanger the loss of his superb elevation by treating us treacherously ? He may write instructions for a son or successor who would doubtless be anxious to distinguish himself in the eyes of a grand nation, but I do not think he intends to break with us himself—at any rate, not in the Russian war. Besides, he has Moscow to revenge if that be his humour.

5th October, 1854.—There seems a great deal of delay in the transmission of official news from the Crimea, or else we should hear of the fall of Sebastopol authentically. How full of bounce and exultation the British Lion is ! How the men up in the little rooms in Printing-house Yard are letting off their crackers—clapping their wings on the safe side of Russia and crowing about *our* power, and *our* success in the Crimea! The article to-day about the widows and orphans is, however, well timed and well written.

10th October, 1854.—Is it not sickening to read of the wholesale mowing down of men at the battle of the Alma? How many families will be bowed down with grief at the sad news! It is, however, to be hoped that the struggle in the Crimea will soon have the effect of bringing matters to a negotiation.

17th October, 1854.—My feet are cold. The fire is gone down. The office is silent after the bustle of the day. The gas-burners shed a complacent look on the vacant stools and desks, where sit the six or eight busy scribblers during the best hours of the day. Could I, with supernatural glance, follow them, and see what they are about, and penetrate their thoughts, a strangely mingled history would, perhaps, in each case, reveal itself. The whole circumstances of even the simplest life would fill an interesting volume. The Recording Angel, whose book I was told of when a small boy, must have plenty to do. Well—my feet don't get warmer, and I want my tea. Let us turn out the complacent burners, and leave the spirits to gaze on the stools and desks. The spirits require no light; to them the night and day are clear alike. Not from the material sun do they receive illumination, but the Light of Lights sheds brightness upon them. May they be granted ministering power to remove temptation from the paths of those whose daily toil it is my duty to superintend, and may they help me also to a blessing!

25th October, 1854.—Yesterday, I accompanied some railway officials down the new junction to the intended Victoria Docks, near Woolwich. They *are* docks, and no mistake; large enough for the largest ships, and fully equal to the extended notions of naval architecture. The entrance-gates will have twenty-seven feet depth of water, and the docks themselves will be perfect lakes. Warehouses, vaults, steam cranes, a railway, and a turnpike road are all marked out, on the most improved plans.

30th October, 1854.—Busy to-day. Away to Haydon Square this afternoon. A jostle through the crowded City—more business than ever. Exuberant street-boys, who whistle in people's ears, and instantly look another way, young swells going home, with the regular Sibthorpe collar, workmen with dirty faces, porters with parcels, anxious middle-aged ladies, careworn shabby young women, sometimes a sweet bright sunbeam of a face in the gloom of the commercial crowd, and now a wanton face, and then an old buffer—all going on; and then, in two or three minutes, all changed for a lot more, still ever changing, flowing unceasingly forward.

25th December, 1854.—Is there not in all of us some kernel of goodness, which, though concealed by our worldly exterior, lives on, amidst our follies and sins, and occasionally expanding to the surface, brings the prayer to our lips, and our knees to the ground? Retiring oft it may be, but destined to stand out revealed when the fleshly covering, with its passions, weaknesses, and misconceptions, shall fade away. Oh, for that time when everybody will be good and pure and bright and glorified! May you and I walk hand-in-hand in that bright kingdom— saved for ever! Until then—the world as it is—and God help us in all things.

4th January, 1855.—On Christmas Day, my foreman, Fogarty, Yeoman of the Guard to the Queen, was nearly squeezed to death between the buffers at this station. As a brakesman was killed a day or two ago, and a boy was run over the night before, one gets quite nervous.

I left poor Fogarty about three o'clock, a fine hearty man, full of life, and I saw him a few hours after, saying his prayers on the hospital bed, with no hope of life. He has, however, lingered on to this time, and now lies with a bare chance of recovery. While I was at the hospital on Christmas night, a man was brought in dead, killed by the train—as they said— at Camden; but I did not know his face, and it appeared afterwards that he lost his life on the North London line, about half-a-mile from Camden.

All the merry time of Christmas, and up to within a day or two, we have been in a sad mess in the station, through increased traffic, the alterations, and want of locomotive power, and my work has been very hard.

Some clever man has invented an improved fog-signal. A fog-signal is a small case of tin, which contains percussion caps and gunpowder, and, being placed on the rail, the pressure of the wheel fires it off with a loud report. The *improved* signal we find, discharges pieces of cast-iron, and wounds the men. A few nights ago, one of the guards was hit in the thigh, and nearly bled to death before medical aid could be obtained. A pointsman has since been cut, and I have called in the improved articles. Talking of bleeding to death, one of my men was riding on an engine a few days ago, eating, with a knife in his hand; a sudden movement of the engine threw him into the tender, and ran the knife into his leg and severed an artery.

What of Peace, and the War, and the mismanagement, and the horror? I don't go altogether with you; though you, no doubt, are better able to "surround" the subject. Perhaps I have caught the popular feeling in some respects, although I detest the bounce and self-reliance of the *vox populi*. Whether the Czar intended to overrun Turkey, and all the world afterwards, or whether Napoleon helped us into the row, or not, I cannot say; but the nation has undertaken to check the Czar in a case of aggression, pretty fairly proved against him, and the nation must do its best, under Providence, to carry out that object. Our disasters must be endured, and patient, but energetic exertion must be made to retrieve the position we have lost. Well, I don't like the subject; I seldom tackle it: it is so complicated, so deplorable in every point of view.

26th January, 1855.—The days go quicker, and the hurry of life increases in speed with me.

I tell you of most of our accidents, so I must not omit the case of signalman Rice, who went up a ladder to light the lamp of the auxiliary signal at Chalk Farm bridge last night. This signal is turned by a man down at the tunnel by means of a wire and a spring; and the man had occasion to turn it at the moment poor Rice was lighting it, and so knocked him off his perch, which broke his thigh and ankle-bone very badly.

Think of Lord John resigning! He'd better go home; he's too hoity-toity by half; but let us hear his explanation. Truly the nation is in a mess. Will you take the government and let me go to the Crimea and put the thing to rights? Well, it will come right. Clench your teeth, O people, and endure. Through the mud, and out of the blood, and from the heaps of her brave sons, dead, but deathless, England will rise to her place in the world. Scourged she may be, but Heaven will not cast her off. Purified and humbled she may be, but the better able to resume her path towards her high destiny will she come forth, shaking from her garments the dust of many of her errors. Crime and folly, pride and hypocrisy, may appear in the indictment of the Recording Angel, but from amidst the mire of sin in which she has struggled and plunged, her right arm has held forth Freedom, Truth and Light, the Gospel to the heathen, a home to the outcast, protection to the weak, and words of comfort and hope to the oppressed; and the God of mercy may hide his face from her for awhile, but he will not utterly desert her in her time of need.

31*st January*, 1855.—*Snow*—in your face and round your hat and on your bosom, and insinuating itself into your boots; on the rails; in the points annoyingly; in holes deceitfully seducing you up to your knees; in balls in the horses' feet,—and they slither and slide and look beseechingly; up against doorways, and down chimneys, in heaps unexpectedly; and more and more coming unrelentingly. That is the state of things to-night.

27*th April*, 1855.—Called out in haste. The 4 p.m. passenger train had run into the temporary siding in the new works and upset the carriages and piled them, one over the other, according to the usual completeness with which the ponderous machines are wont to kick up their heels when they do get a chance. Miraculous though it may seem, nobody was hurt. The passengers were fished out of the doors of the carriages. In an hour's time they were all sent away on their journey. A few hours more sufficed to clear the line, and the place looked ready to take its solemn oath that no accident had occurred at all.

I have had a peep at the Emperor of the French and his pretty wife. She is a blue-eyed quiet-looking lady. His expression is glum and lachrymose. The carriage stopped in front of me. Prince Albert's open handsome face was better worth seeing than all the rest. Two of my brothers-in-law had tickets for the interior of the Crystal Palace, and they describe the scene as thrilling in the extreme. I went into the building after the departure of the Royal personages. The company, the building, and the glorious objects of interest create awe rather than delight in me. The busts of the great men of all ages, the temples and other structures in exact imitation of those used by the ancients thousands of years ago, the representations of forgotten art, &c., drag from the dust of ages, in unexpected vividness, the Past, stripping it of its misty imaginative veil and exposing it in almost abrupt reality to the mind; while the glory of the Present, in the living plants and the thronging people, the sparkling water, the hum of voices, and the heart-thrilling music— not forgetting the refreshment department, together with the shining walls of the fairy-like building, with the bright sun pouring its delighted rays through the sparkling crystal, on objects of grace and beauty everywhere. All this floods my heart and makes me fear for the aspiring pride of man, when he contemplates as much of the present, accumulated and combined with the past, lest he forget the fate of Babylon. All the while the Future mingles with my reflections, and the fear of what is to be at length subsides into a warm thankfulness and an earnest trust in Him whose glory and majesty are shown forth in all these things. Thus I lean as a little child on the wonderful Creator and am content. All this flits through my mind while I smile at a joke from my brothers or beat time to some recognised air.

4th May, 1855.—Last night the fireman of our night shunting engine was found in one of the signalman's huts in a state of intoxication, with his head under the grate; and shortly afterwards the signalman himself was discovered, on his back, on the line, nearly as bad; and further down the line a hamper which had been stolen from a down goods train, and evidently mistaken for a hamper of wine, was also found. The contents were, however, drugs. One bottle contained essential oil of almonds. What the bottle contained which these men drank from is yet a mystery. I should think it was spirits of wine, by the quick effect upon them.

A few hours previous to this one of our oldest porters was caught between the waggons and horribly crushed.

These incidents occupied the night foreman a long time, and when he went back to the office he found that the day foreman had left a pet monkey in the place, and the little brute had got at some brandy and was completely drunk. When I saw the animal in the morning he was looking very lugubrious and like a certain superior animal under similar circumstances. His master informed me that he ate two packets of blacking and a box of pills a few days ago.

7th May, 1855.—At the opera. All the men with stiff necks, drawling gentlemanly voices, white kids, and an air which seemed to express their satiated familiarity with the whole thing. The ladies all handsome—for fine feathers do make fine birds—brilliants, bare necks, and teeth like a sunbeam.

10th May, 1855.—Sir, I am elected a Vestryman of the great parish of St. Pankridge. Sir, I am now a member of the local legislative body, and I do trust that it will not be necessary for me to point to this stunning fact at any future period of our intercourse, when you might thoughtlessly be inclined to presume upon the urbanity with which I have treated you up to this "ripping" point of my career. I can now sympathise with the Emperor under the circumstances of his sudden elevation from poverty to power, although my progress into distinction has been somewhat more gradual than his. Sir, you will not feel hurt at these remarks. They are the stern voice of duty coming from a heart overflowing with love to my species, be they ever so humble. You, sir, are humble; I was humble; but you will reflect that the cares of government are now heavy on my shoulder. Think of me as the gentle youth with whom you roamed the Yorkshire heather and the Hampstead hills, and forget the grave brow of the local senator. Remember the wanderings of yore, the drives and the dinners, the confidings, the conversations, the cabs, the warmth of the grip which no storm hath relaxed; but, confound it, Sir! no liberties with a Vestryman.

18th May, 1855.—I attended the Vestry Hall on Wednesday last and took my seat. It is good fun. I shall enjoy the debates. There is something to be learnt in all new branches of business; but this will combine amusement with knowledge. An old "bloke"—a barrister and churchwarden—took the chair. He makes a good speech. There is a Dissenting minister, who is an active member, and there are two or three more barristers, a portly tailor who wears a moustache, one or two publicans, and a lot of rummy-looking silent members, who afford me some occupation to think what the dickens they are. There are swellish vestrymen, shabby vestrymen (decidedly so—awkward boots and home-made trousers, and all that kind of thing), vestrymen with unexceptionable white shirts and collars, and vestrymen who do not show either shirt or collar, it being Wednesday, the day before clean-shirt day; which is a pity. As I am known to represent the interests of the London and North-Western Railway I am treated with some consideration.

28th May, 1855.—One of the lads attached to my office, a promising youth of sixteen, the pet of his mother, went out yesterday in a boat at Richmond, and was drowned. Poor lad! all my office is in great gloom to-day. He was much liked. How grief-stricken his bereaved parents must be.

7th June, 1855.—Do you remember my telling you of a man named Baker who realised a fortune at share-speculating and kept his brougham and had a beautiful wife? Well, he came down—lost, lost, lost—and finally purloined a Turkish bond, was arrested, but escaped to America. Hearing that his wife was in the hospital very ill, he returned and obtained a situation, was met and taken into custody, and was sentenced to a term of imprisonment in Newgate, where he now lies; while his beautiful wife lies stark and dead in the Middlesex Hospital.

1st July, 1855.—What think you of Lord Robert Grosvenor's Bill? I approve of it. The putting a stop to the Sunday morning trading is much required. It will oblige masters to pay their men in time for them to get their Sunday provisions overnight, and it will oblige men to go home and give their wives some money, instead of going direct from work to the public-house, whence they do not turn out until they have arrived at drunkenness and midnight. We much want a series of measures to keep back the mob from encroaching on the Sunday. The line must be kept better or it will be entirely broken, like the course after a race, and the thimble-riggers, the dancers, the singers will commence their business, and the whole uproar of Vanity Fair will arise on the green sward lately so serene and clear. The observance of Sunday as a religious day may probably not be directly ordered in the New Testament Scriptures, but even as a human institution it is most valuable. Who in this busy world, with any religion at all, does not feel the necessity of one day in seven to recruit his weary mind, to collect his hurried and scattered thoughts, and to kneel calmly in prayer for his neighbours, his country, the whole world, and himself? Who that has felt any pleasure in this exercise is not convinced, by any occasional deprivation of it, that without the day of holy rest he would dwindle into a mere machine, with blunted sympathies and bewildered thoughts, hopeless and without consolation? Let us stand by the Sunday.

31*st July*, 1855.—To-day I had business at the Marylebone Police Court. While I waited I surveyed the poor wretches who were about to be taken before the magistrate. Here is a labouring man with a damaged nose and swollen lips. Drink and fighting appeared to be his weaknesses. A poor careworn woman brings him a bottle of ginger-beer to cool his feverish throat. She is doubtless his wife and is seeing him through it. There sit two boys, about sixteen years of age; one short and stumpy, with pent brows, sore eyes, and an underhung jaw; the other, thin and delicate-looking, with regular features, but a crooked smile, and bad teeth. Poor lads!—in the grand summing-up of this world's complicated Case, how much of your vice and frailty will fall away from you to swell the indictment of those who have neglected you—be they parents, or parishioners, or the nation at large! Yonder is a drunken woman, about forty or more, with remains of beauty in her red face. She is scarcely sober, and takes it into her head to administer a box on the ear to a rather bumptious policeman. A commotion ensues. Then there is a cavil between a half-tipsy Irishman, all rags and dirt, and the before-mentioned policeman, whom I feel inclined to report for his taunts and gibes to the prisoners. Sitting near are two of the lowest description of prostitutes, one of them slim and pretty, and the other a plain stumpy little termagant, both wearing a defiant expression in their young eyes. Now comes in an old lady, with a terrible black eye. She is accompanied by her daughter, a young lady with a veil and her hair done up. Some wretch, I suppose, has given the mamma a pop in the eye and she attends to prosecute. But enough!

11th August, 1855.—Talk of Busmen. Can't anything be done for them? They commence work at about 8 a.m., and leave off at midnight. On Sundays from 10 a.m., to past midnight. "Do you ever see a Bible?" said a parson to one of them the other day. "Why, yes, I *sees* em," said the man, "cos there's my six children has one a-piece; but that's as fur as I gets. Why, love yer art, sir, wen I goes straight home—cos there's many as don't—well, by the time I sits down it's half arter twelve, and wen I tries it on to look at the paper I'm asleep afore you can say 'knife.' So I gives the paper to my misses and I ses to her, ses I, 'you take that—I'll smoke.' Readin's done wi' me, and I've done wi' readin. Why, sir, sixty mile a day in the open air does it. You can't stand a close room arterwards—you're safe to fall asleep. Not but what I've gone to church twice a-day, five years at a stretch, right off, when I was a gennelman's servant. But I can't bear to think about it. Look out, Bill!" Stout gentleman at this juncture rushes out of a brewery and blows up the busman for stopping up the road, so that the drays are detained. "For my part," says the gentleman, "I wish you and the cabs were under heavy fines." "Oh, you do, do yer?" replies the bus-driver. "Well, them brewers ain't the cream-o-the-valley, *I* can see." And so the remainder of the ride is not sociable.

22nd August, 1855.—

> Accursed, subtle, tempting evil!
> Thou fluid extract of the devil!
> Avaunt—begone—and ne'er again
> Beguile my lips to steal my brain
> The flower of life, forced by thy heat,
> Blooms bright and ruddy, high and sweet,
> Our hands the friendly grasp return,
> The fires of passion fiercely burn,
> Valour and wit escape control,
> And pleasure dances round the bowl.
> But Oh! the morning sees the bloom
> All spent,—all wasted the perfume.
> The trembling hands relax their hold,
> The fire of love is dead and cold,
> Dismay sits grim on valour's stool,
> And wit stares now a vacant fool,
> And Hell yawns round the broken bowl.

20th November, 1856.—The London and North Western Railway Company have appointed me Goods Manager of the Southern District.

29th November, 1856.—A letter from Thomas Carlyle, the author, about his packages. He writes a fist as queer as his style.

11th December, 1856.—Dined out twice lately, everything tempting and glittering; but a comfortable dinner at home beats it all.

22nd December, 1856.—Do you believe this? It is said that the new electric telegraph was tried on a new line in Wales the other day, but immediately the clerk attempted to spell on the instrument one of the many-consonanted Welsh names, one of the wires curled up and the other broke off short!

16th June, 1858.—The sun is setting gloriously over old Camden, as he will set, Robin Adair, when some one else fills this chair of mine, and when you have ceased to bewail your erring flock and some other chap is going through the same performance. Meanwhile, we will hope that no greater trouble than has hitherto befallen us may come between us and the end, and that a peaceful ray of the wondrous luminary may fall on the green turf of our graves and gild the tear of pleasant memory, shed by the friend whose love recalls us, while our pardoned spirits rest in Heaven, through the same goodness and mercy which have followed us all the days of our lives.

9th August, 1858.—As regards Canada, if that dream be realised, then, Robin Adair,

>You shall come over there
>And preach on the stair,
>Or the barrel of beer.
>To my wife and her dear,
>In our dwelling so fair,
>Where Loo and her little-ones ever shall be
>In clover and ease till they lie down and dee;
>And folks in the future shall tell—and no lee—
>That once in those parts lived a Bob and Davie,
>Two out-and-out fellows as ever could be,
>And that many a year they lived jollily
>In England, the land away over the sea,
>The home of the Briton, the soil of the free;
>And that when they came out into West Canadee
>They brought sons and daughters—how many? Let's see
>Never mind! but they finally left ninety-three.

19th August, 1858.—Milverton—Somersetshire.

I have just been standing in the moonlight in front of your old domicile at Milverton. It is a beautiful old place certainly, only not quite so large as I expected to see it. The church looks romantic in the moonbeams. The sweet-toned bell struck nine as I strolled round the venerable fabric, full of dreams of the past. I had a little difficulty in finding poor Mary Ann's grave. It is situated in a peaceful spot. Now I have returned to mine inn to write to you and Eliza. What a glorious country it is all about here! I wish you were with me to answer the thousand questions which arise in my mind. No one seems to know anything. The landlord don't remember anything, and he hasn't been long here. The waiter tells me long yarns about everything *but* Milverton; and the folk seem to think I am not much good, prowling about in the dark. Never mind, I have seen the place and am satisfied; but I hope the sheets at the hotel won't be damp. Such brandy!—none of your foreign stuff—real British, and no mistake. Bah! I repeat, I hope the sheets won't be damp.

17th September, 1858.—I have been to the Isle of Man; wasn't sick going or coming. Like the place; pretty country, like Wicklow. Town stinks of drains when the tide is out, and of fish when it's in. People talk a sort of Irish brogue. Went to church, where they collected the money for the poor in an apparatus resembling a warming pan. To the play, where I saw 'Macbeth' with a vengeance. Didn't sleep much o'nights, owing to a church clock just outside my bedroom window striking the hours cruelly loud.

3rd October, 1858.—Sunday.—It is now about half-past seven, and you, I presume, are sowing broadcast in the field of your Master. May your arm be strong, and the grain full of fructifying vigour, sinking deep into the heart, to bring forth abundantly. Tell your flock how responsible they are; shew them the wonderful miracle of a life—its grand mechanism—its wonderful sustenance—the beauty of its youth—the mighty productions of its manhood—its certain decay, and then the mocking infirmities of age—all speaking with eloquent force, to the thinking mind, that such a glorious creation as man could not have been made to run a purposeless course. Bid them work while it is yet day, each one assisting, in his sphere, the step or goodness for which each generation is collectively answerable. Call on them to fight the evil which all must feel to exist in their hearts ; to cultivate the heavenly inclination to goodness, even if it be but a spark, the minute remnant of their divine origin. Entreat them to fan that spark into a flame until it illumines the whole character. Picture to them the hatefulness of sin, and make them to feel the consoling truth that when the wicked man turneth away from his wickedness and doeth that which is lawful and right he shall save his soul alive. The tender mercy of an earthly parent who loves his darlings may feebly convey to them the idea of the ready forgiveness of Him of whom you are commissioned to speak. Pardon for the past, grace and strength for the future, you can offer in His name ; and it will go hard, my anxious pastor, if you do not here and there reclaim some wandering soul.

29th July, 1859.—The Trosachs.—Here you are, or, at least, here I am! I have come by Callander from Stirling, and coached it from Callander. I have just now taken a long walk up Glenfinlas—so grand and solemn—swelling bully-looking mountains, that seem to defy and mock the notion of anyone climbing up their sides—rushing, roaring, dashing waters—and such oppressive loneliness. Altogether I felt an indefinite fear as the twilight drew in, especially when I came to a spot where the rocks echoed the hollow sound of the waterfall a hundred times.

The daylight remains here much later than in the south, as you probably know, and the outline of the mountains against the twilight is very beautiful.

I start for Loch Katrine to-morrow morning. I shall go up it and on to Inversnaid, and down Loch Lomond to Balloch and Glasgow.

I enjoyed the sight of picturesque Edinburgh; likewise I smelled the smells of the old town, down about the Cowgate. I did Arthur's Seat and all the sights, Portobello and bathing into the bargain.

At tea here this evening I fell in with a chatty pleasant lady from Gateshead. Now, hold hard! her husband is with her. He seems a decent old chap, but he has a hair lip and articulates with difficulty; moreover, he is troubled with eructations, saving your presence, and looks the next minute as though he had discharged an agreeable duty to his fellow creatures. They have just gone to bed. They are going my way to-morrow. The old chap smokes a cigar, so we shall probably fraternise, for, truth to tell, I am not enamoured of my own company on a trip of this kind. I'd give a brass "farden" if my little woman and you were with me.

At the present juncture I am writing, and smoking a cigar, and I've a tumbler of toddy before me, and there's a gent opposite "as is doin' of the same," barring the writing. On my left is a long-nosed dogmatical Britisher, who has just shut up a long-winded lot of bosh about Louis Napoleon, and further on there is a young "feller" who has been walking his feet off up the "mountings" and looks done up. We are rather a different lot of "gents" from those who were in the habit of prowling about here a hundred years ago, and if it were as cold here then as now, I should think that the absence of breeches must have been felt severely.

I find that there's no post from these parts until to-morrow night, and then the time is uncertain, so I shall carry this in my pocket until I reach civilisation. I may add something more to-morrow, but it will probably be in Gaelic, as you know how readily I forget my native tongue.

13*th December*, 1861.—I believe you are right as to the £150 days. I don't see much more money, and I don't think I am happier. The latter commodity is, I suppose, nearly equally distributed, or, at any rate, much more so than we think generally. I have, no doubt, as much pleasure, if one could get through, and push aside the pride, affectation and bosh, and arrive at the real state of one's condition—which is difficult to do—I dare say I think myself a very important man of business— that I am working out my little bit of duty in the world; and that your portraiture of me, although jocularly put, is in reality true, and I am a most excellent fellow, notwithstanding certain remembrances of errors and shortcomings which will come up. I find myself uncommonly willing to take a favourable view of myself at all times.

The religious meeting was a breakfast in the shops at Euston a Sunday or two ago, at which nearly 400 men of ours assembled. They were addressed by Canon Champneys, Judge Payne, and others, and the speeches were eloquent exhortations to the men to consider their religious responsibility as men, parents, and christians. If no lasting good has arisen, the effort was an earnest one to promote christianity, and was sensibly and temperately carried out. I don't admire the greasy whining 'parties' who grow out of a certain method of teaching religion. No; goodness in act and deed, evidencing love in the heart, and a true imitation of the Great Example, the kind and pure Christ, I like to recognize and cheer on; and I find such men amongst all denominations and in many unexpected places.

I am going to Folkestone on Tuesday. Why not come up and go with me? We would gaze together into the impatient billows, which lick, like faithful mastiffs, the smiling cliffs of dear old Albion. We would pour the libation to old ocean. We would wander on the pebbly strand and forget awhile the world and our work. These balmy days, so unlike December's usual rigour, ought to beguile us into thoughts of spring-time, while our voices, gently harmonising with the far down murmur of the waves, should pleasantly break the sea-side solitude. Old memories would then arise of days gone grey in our poor recollections, and scenes from the Magic Lantern of the past would be lighted up to touch the chords of our old hardened hearts.

30*th January*, 1863.—Many thanks for all your good wishes. I think 1863 looks hopeful. I begin it more cheerfully, in many respects, than I did 1862. That period will be long remembered: it has been a 'fizzer.' Yet who can reflect on even the darkest pages of his existence without being able to thank the great Disposer of events for many mercies? Pardon me for trespassing on your line of business for the moment.

Is Harris still with you?

> Then let the Harris busy be
> In Wybunbury's bowers,
> And roar, and laugh, and preach, and spree,
> And waste the vicar's hours.

> But, Parson, on the other side
>   Of his great mouth, I ween,
> He smiles when o'er the wincing boys
>   He lifts his awful cane.
> No laugh for them from him the " brute, "
>   No spree, no jolly air.
> 'Hi ! you young sir, that thing won't suit !'
>   He says, as from his chair
> He starts—rage in his eye—and all
>   The boys around he beats !
> Ah me ! indeed it doth appal
>   To know mankind are cheats.

September, 1863.—Jersey. A soft wind ripples the paper on which I write; the sun-glare is occasionally relieved by a cloud; the sea breaks on the strand beneath me in subdued waves, and in a majesty of expanse stretches far away to the verge of the horizon. Of late it tore and foamed and dashed, in mighty waves, rushing to the shore with greedy breakers, ravenous to swallow up the land; again and again thrust back, to return again with renewed strength. Now its calm bosom gently heaves. The giant sleeps.

We are greatly enjoying ourselves here and gathering strength for the next year's campaign. But even here there is excitement; for just now I had to descend from my perch on a rock to bully a man who was going too near my hen and chickens, who were bathing in a neighbouring nook in the rocks. I resume my meditations and return along the sands, very much like the sea I have mentioned—calmer after a 'boil over'.

These parts are very beautiful : such pretty bays and wild rocks and old castles. I roam about in drab boots and an old grey coat, and feel quite easy.

25th September, 1863.—On South Western Railway.—I have just passed Winchester, flying at the rate of twenty miles an hour towards Southampton. The sun shines over the green landscape, and I am enjoying the ride. On my left sits a plain young lady in black, and on my right a civil gentleman, who lent me his 'Times.' Whither are we three going? Shall we ever sit side by side for three hours again? What is she? What is he? They may be a prince and princess, or the proprietors of a tripe shop. What a trio, presently to throw and dissolve itself in different directions! What a shell thrown into Southampton, to break up into scattered particles to do mischief !

7.30 p.m.—Now I am in the carriage with my brood going t
London, having met them at the Jersey boat, given them some
grub, looked after the luggage, and lodged them safely here.
They all look brown and healthy, although the children have
been very sick on the voyage. Away we go, homeward; another
happy holiday spent; another bright summer's pleasure off our
lives. *Sic transit, &c.*

10.30 p.m.—Home. Greetings with Ellen. Hot supper.
Running about the house. Enquiries after the dog and the goat
and the cat and the rabbit. Item, heavy cab fare.

27th September, 1863.—Great Berkhampstead. I am seated
on the gnarled root of a tree. In front of me are hundreds of
rose-trees, each with its particular last rose of summer; and
beyond lies, outstretched, Ashridge Park and the usual green and
rich country of old England. I have breakfasted, but the
household is not yet down, and I have come out for a sniff of the
pure air.

Poor F, who was Station-master at ———, is here. The
disease in his bones does not abate much. He may linger for a
year or two, but it is thought that recovery is out of the question.
His sufferings are great. How ashamed one feels of grumbling
and discontent when such a case as this young fellow's comes
before one. It is comforting to believe that in the next world the
perplexing inequalities of destiny which exist here will all be
adjusted.

25th October, 1863.—Sunday.—It is a great blessing, this
Sunday rest. The care and strife, the ambitions and humiliations
are suspended, and one has time to pause on this landing of Life's
staircase and quiet the poor torn and weary spirit. The good
words of the preacher haul in the slack of our practice and bring
about reflection. The prayers tranquilise us and revive forgotten
hopes of that sweet world to which the pardoned are journeying.
There is time to be oneself. The gas of the world, which has
puffed up thoughtless impulses, and carried us high away into the
clouds of danger and temptation, is turned off for the day, and we
walk on *terra firma*. The sins of the week descend also with our
balloon and lie in their deformity around us. We gaze and
deplore and resolve ; and, remembering former deplorings and

resolutions, pray for better strength, feeling the value of the Great Sacrifice.

12th November, 1863.—Here I am waiting at Guildhall. The Queen sent to me and John Doe greeting, commanding me to appear in the Court of Exchequer here with a 36-pounder cannon, about which there is a dispute in law—the cannon being in my possession officially. So here I am with my cannon. Doe has not yet turned up. I suppose he is a relative of Gog and Magog and other myths.

It is mouldy work dawdling about. The Court has an ancient, not to say a fish-like smell; so I don't go in there much. All sorts of people hang about; many of them greasy, with bags, and with their trousers fringed at the heels. Everybody looks ugly somehow, and one has a general distrust of all who come near. This is unchristian, but irresistible. The judges at these Courts have all been changed since I first attended them. The old faces have passed away, and I only recognise an old barrister at the bar here and there. There is M., a rising young barrister within my remembrance. He is now a sad old guy, with white hair and a fearful stand-up collar. He only wants a chair and two bearers, to complete him, and he would take no end of money for fireworks. Ah me! how the time and the people pass away,—and I, too, cannot be standing on a pedestal witnessing the onward movement. No—we are all in the current—moving surely, though imperceptibly.

7th December, 1863.—Ted has just been relating how a man he heard of never bought any coals, never had any given him, and never stole any—yet always had plenty in his cellar. It appears that his garden wall was alongside a canal, and his plan was to place on the top of the wall a glass bottle. Playful bargees with freights of coal could not resist a cock-shy, and, with no ammunition but coal, they used that freely. The old man on the other side of the wall picked up and bagged the shots, replacing the bottle when necessary, which was not often.

1st April, 1864.—I have had a few days of freedom from toothache and some bothers which are my thorns in the flesh, and I have been happy and grateful, enjoying this (on the whole) most agreeable world; laying in a little stock to remember when the clouds come,—antidotes to murmuring,—stores of consolation when the porter's knot has to be put on to carry the burdens of this jolly old eccentric pilgrimage.

11*th April*, 1864.—Garibaldi is struggling through London to-day. People who have been to see the progress say he only reached Kensington about 5 o'clock, and, considering the sea of people in Pall Mall, at Charing Cross, etc., he will, I should think, be at Stafford House about next Monday, if he has luck.

16*th September*, 1864.—I went to the Adelphi Theatre this week and saw Toole, a wonderful actor; but, Robin, we don't roar, as we used, at fun. Alas! that organ is getting weak in the wind— the hot summers, the heat of the day, has dried up the green verdure—and if we are wiser (which I question) we are sadder. I hope we shall be able to keep a few grins to the end, however.

18*th October*, 1864.—Mr. C. Mason is away on a tour, and I am "taking the duty" for him. A lull in the business leaves me listening to the clock ticking on the mantel-piece—a sound which seems to be elected to the chair when there is a general meeting of silence.

20*th February*, 1865.—In the York and Albany just now, at my luncheon, I came across a fellow slightly cranky. He talked of the fresh air, the bad cooking of the chop, his literary labours, the clubs, the insignificance of money to him, though not a rich man, the state of his health, the death of Cardinal Wiseman, the absurdity of men looking into their hats at church; cried because he had lost his wife, "sometime ago, of course", and then laughed at Punch, and at Protestant parsons; declaimed against the taking of "our abbeys" by the Protestants; and wound up by prophesying vehemently that England would be Roman Catholic in less than fifty years.

Musn't I be short of news when I write such a paragraph as the above? Well, one has nothing to say; the freshness is wearing off, I suppose, and we don't see the fun of little matters as we did formerly, or, at least, we fear to write about them, to bore our friends withal, as of old.

What think you of the weather? It is a neat old-fashioned winter, I submit; and those who have been talking of "good old seasonable weather" have, I trust, got plenty of it this time.

For my part, I have had enough. I want a little piece of soft weather, when you can get out of bed without feeling as though you had taken strychnine—when a man may walk to his small clothes without destroying his dignity by making hideous grimaces in the presence of his weaker vessel—and when shaving isn't quite a process of refined torture.

19th September, 1865.—We have had to kill poor old Floss, our doggie. We could not cure his fleas, and they were migrating all over the house; and so there was a long parting, and the sound of his cheery bark went away from us, as all things will go, I suppose, in time. Verily you might take a worse subject for your sermon than that poor little affectionate bevermined dog. . Do the beasts perish?—Are you sure? · If so, there is many a beautiful spirit which could be profitably transferred into the carcass of a man, in exchange for his own—so far as my feeble vision can see of the matter.

1st October, 1865.—How imperceptibly the hand goes round the dial! Our seniors are gradually slipping from the front rank, and we shall soon have to totter to their places, to gaze into eternity, face to face. The hands of those who climbed the ladder of life before us, and which have so long been extended downwards to help our steps, are rapidly disappearing into the clouds; and we must hold each rung ourselves, and in our turn cheer on those beneath us.

—*October*, 1865[*].

> Who came between the 'tin' and me
> By dodges which I couldn't see,
> And with the plate made much too free?
>   H.B.
>
> Who knew that I was far too pure
> To wish with gold Life's ills to cure,
> And that I relished being poor?
>   H.B.
>
> Who for my sake lost self respect,
> And to be thief did not object,
> That I on gold might not be wreck'd?
>   H.B.
>
> Who coloured well, with reasoning smile,
> To doting ears, the artful wile
> That would my expectations 'spile'?
>   H.B.
>
> For this and all, we'd *strike the lyre*,
> H. B., my boy, and raise thee higher
> With patent rope, and end with fire,
>   H.B.

---

[*] My friend was swindled by H.B. out of some property. A little was saved, but nearly destroyed afterwards in an accidental fire.

8th February, 1866.—Waif-like, I am rushing to and fro on the earth. In No. 135 carriage, Great Northern Railway, I am firing away to Peterborough, while you live at home at ease and, I dare say, at this instant are devoutly giving your blessing to some excellent tax-collector, or other person, who relieves you of your filthy lucre. I am thinking how cleanly you and I must naturally be. We seem to get rid of that kind of filth by natural instinct, until really sometimes we are uncomfortably clean in that respect—cleaned out, in fact.

28th March, 1866.—Splendid day here yesterday. I went into the country to look at a coal wharf, and lingered in the lanes listening to the wonders of the birds, and breathing the sunshine. I had had a week of toothache and was free from it, and I felt all the sweet influences of the returning season with doubled happiness. Will there be singing birds, and winding lanes, and fair meadows in the place whither thou art guiding us, O my Preacher? Take thou mine hand and lead me on quickly, for I tire of struggling men and roaring cities. I never loved the strife, and in the battle with sin I have ever bitten the dust. My heart yearns for the quiet of that tranquil world where men and women are as the angels.

29th June, 1866.—As regards the war between Austria and Italy, my commonplace order of mind wanders down below the inflated speeches and proclamations of ambitious kings and politicians, who, in the pursuit of their game, are blind to all other considerations. I find my way, mole-like, below the grandeur and the glory, and the hollow appeals to romance and humbug, and I get to poor lads, torn away from honest productive occupations, and to mothers and sisters, and aunts, and wives and cousins, and the great heap of accumulated grief which these gilded and silvered and feathered kings and kaisers are making amongst thousands of human beings. Could the suffering of one battle-field—the stark dead and the parched wounded—the agony of all those who wait the fate of a son or brother or husband—could such things be numbered up and divided to the accounts of those who cause the war, the weight would take them all to the bottom of the bottomless pit, or keep them going down for ever.

10*th November*, 1866.—Rugby. This is a pleasant place; house, high and dry, in a field off the road; a mile-and-a-half from the station; town, half-way; good suburbs; town, clean; good shops. Now for good, sweet, juicy apples: I think at this place, we are equalled by few and surpassed by none; and for pigs that will try the olfactory nerves with here and there one, I think I may venture to put in a modest claim. Good garden, fish-pond, &c. Our pony is a pretty fellow, eats sugar and apples, and is a great favourite. But oh! you won't betray me if I tell you that I have a dreadful secret respecting that quadruped? My friend! what are my feelings when my wife and family are fondling that pony, and calling my attention to his beauties— while I smile a ghastly deception, for I know, oh! I know, that the beggar is as old as Methuselah, and that I paid for him just twice as much as he is worth. Sold he was—sold I was—and sold they were!

I go to town several times during the month, but I can get home at night very well, and even to dinner, for we have taken to dining late. Dinner at six, a cup of coffee at nine, and by ten we are lying all unconscious in a dark house on a hill-side, the sleeping birds, the trees, and hedges, and growing crops, and the shining stars, out in the night all around us,—until that bright "Fo-e-bus" drives up his carriage to the gates of day, and lets the silent Lady Morn alight; who, clad in silver sheen, with solemn tread advances to relieve the watching stars, and bid the world arise.

Nearly thirty years ago I went to Hampstead, and a few days past I came away from it. All the while I have loved it, lived near it, watched its changes and the falling out, one by one, of its old familiar faces; and now mine has dropped away from it. The persons I knew as acquaintances will gradually fade from my ken; and many, whom I knew only by sight, from youth to manhood, or from manhood to old age, and whose familiar passings, though we never spoke, are a thing of regret now, will soon be forgotten and know me no more. I clung much of late to all the old views and scenes, and took many a long walk to indulge my memory. I shall see the "pleasant hill" many a time yet, I hope; but I have ceased to be an *habitué* and the link is fractured, if not quite broken.

30th December, 1866.—Another year is falling over into the gulf, and before it passes away, I write to congratulate you and myself on the many blessings which have befallen to you and me, and to yours and mine, during the course of it. Chequered it has been, as its predecessors were, and as, probably, its successors will be, if we live; but goodness and mercy have been prominent throughout. For which, my dear old chap, let us heartily thank God.

A—— and J—— came down to spend Christmas with us, so that we were all round the same table on that day of family gatherings. Charlie and his wife and family joined us, and we were jolly. It was a scene worth looking at, when Charlie performed some of his wonders. All the fresh and shining faces of the youngsters, and the happy laughter of the others, including the servants, the shepherd, and the farm groom, and a bucolic friend. The applause was genuine, and Charlie was king of the jollity. We ate and drank of good Christmas things, we talked soberly, but pleasantly, of old times, and old places, and old friends, and remembered tenderly dear old seniors departed. We sang a little, and romped a little, and played cards a little, and slept soundly after it all; placing the day in our memories with a red letter.

I hope you enjoyed the day equally. How are you all? Will "Sally come up" to this place? It isn't London; but, mind you, Rugby is not to be sneezed at—although our refreshment rooms don't come up to the wants and wishes of cold, tired, ill-tempered, and over-pampered travelling authors, who, in a Christmas book, which should be all charity and forgiveness, choose to wound and pain poor hard-working women, who have to stand all day in the draught, about which Mr. Dickens is so funny, and to put up with the insolence and impudence of the British Public, who, be it said with all deference, is too often rude to young persons behind a counter. Nevertheless, Rugby is a neat, clean town, with good shops, and gentlemanly boys, and civil tradesmen, and an excellent church choir, which my daughter is about to join:—

"He hears his daughter's voice
Singing in the village choir,
And it makes his heart rejoice."

And then we have our performing pony and the chance of a spill any time you ride out; besides the excitement, occasionally, of onion fairs, and horse fairs, and circuses, and the celebrated Japanese Tommy, and always, of an evening, the unparalleled society of this young fellow. Oh, yes! Sairey must come; besides, I want to hear her say her catechism—being her god-father.

A CHRISTMAS CAROL.

"And there were in the same country shepherds abiding in the field, keeping watch over their flocks * * * and the glory of the Lord shone round about them."

> A shepherd I—these sheep of mine
> Are on Christ's birthday found
> Within my fold—and glories shine
> In blessings all around.
>
> For Goodness crowning all my days,
> Which Mercy doth afford,
> Thy Name to glorify and praise
> My heart inclines, O Lord.
>
> Unto the Saviour lead the way
> Of this Thy flock, and mine;
> O guide us here, Lord, that we may
> Join that bright Host of Thine.

—*January*, 1867.—The generations passing away, one after the other, in what may seem a meaningless succession, the curiously teeming earth, full of living things, the wondrous creations in earth and air and sea, the far-off worlds, and all the mighty things which have passed before our eyes on our puny little journey have not explained themselves to us—we know nothing of their object, nor why so much labour has been expended, the result of much of which seems to us to "waste its sweetness." They have, however, humbled our thoughts. They announce themselves as the works of the overwhelmingly great Creator; and in all of them His mercy and benevolence, His beauty and glory, shine forth. We are glad to leave the position of carping spectators, and to fall into the ranks as a part of the great family of so good and tender a Father. We remember that He has known us from the first moment of our existence until now—all our thoughts, and sins, and repentance, and motives—and that He considers that we are but flesh; and we cast ourselves unreservedly into His hands, and so rise up and pursue our way. If the vast creation do not satisfy our craving after the designs of God, we must be content and trust Him. If the mysterious life and death of Jesus Christ, the need of so great a sacrifice at all, the slow process of the belief in Him, and the doubts and fears which beset at times even the best of Christians, do not explain themselves, we must submit and trust Him. That Christ came, and left us an example of pure living, and executed His divine mission in sorrow and death, leaving us tender words of consolation for all periods of life, and that He fulfilled a scheme of mercy for mankind is certain. But as I get down the hill, and ponder on all that I have been permitted to see. I feel confident that the plan has far greater influence and efficacy than some of our brethren are willing to attribute to it. I dwell upon the complicated causes of sin and wickedness, and the nice shades of guilt to be shared and appropriated, and I think of all my poor brothers lying on the surface of this globe; and then, in warm sympathy for that class of created beings in which it has pleased God to place me, I pray for all sorts and conditions of men. A perfect Man came upon earth and was our brother. His highest attribute was compassion. His words breathed mercy. Then not alone for thee, my poor, blinded, bigoted brother, nor for you alone, O man of severe countenance, died He. If the condition be repentance, then who shall fix the quantity of that precious thing? May not one electric atom, as the soul escapes, be sufficient to bring it into the boundless domain of that mercy which seems to be a part of everything we know of God? For myself, I know the worthless thing sin has made of this curiously constructed body which the Almightly has entrusted to my care. I feel that if He were to call me to account for my stewardship I should be condemned. But He knows that I love Him, and that at times, fitful and rare indeed, and followed by long periods of partial forgetfulness, I have given some indications of a disposition not unmindful of His great goodness to me and my fellow-creatures. Feeling myself nothing, therefore, but a man anxious for God's mercy, in any form that his mysterious and wonderful ways may please to bestow it upon me, I proceed to walk the rest of the road, more circumspectly perhaps, though I know what little trust there is to be put in my watchfulness, but still hopeful that the same goodness will attend me that has followed me hitherto; and when the end comes I shall not regret to quit the perplexing world, although I shall remember lovingly the happiness and affection I have enjoyed therein. But something within tells me there is a better place whither all will come—and I am content to go as I came, at His will and command.

29th April, 1867.—A—— and J—— have been spending a fortnight with us. We are walking calmly forward, we trust with becoming dignity and a deep sense of our position, to the venerable titles of grandfather and grandmother. We are well aware that it would be vain to offer any remonstrance to that unrelenting old gentleman called Time; but I feel, my dear young friend, that it would afford me unqualified relief if I could be permitted to give him one good hit.

15th April, 1869.—
> In the early train, in the rising morning,
> Passing by the meadows, through the balmy air,
> I began a letter unto you, my Turnbull,
> In the usual manner, beautiful and rare.
> But I broke my pencil, rushing by the streams,
> Racing past the swallows, gliding as in dreams,
> And I fell a-musing as I sped away
> From the gloomy tunnel, plunging into day,
> And you lost effusions born of morning beams.

I read Sally's letter to Bob last night. That is a treat he gives me sometimes. Her quaint fun reads to me as though it were "a diary of a lady of the blank century found" somewhere. She is brimful of humour, like a house with Venetian blinds—undemonstrative without, but full of merriment and music within —glorious when the door opens on the dark night.

Bob has a £10 rise in his salary, passed to-day: £36 per annum. Awful sum! Do you recollect when you received that stipend? How you looked upon a man with £100 per annum as an aristocrat, and with thoughts of what a person you would be when your income should reach that amount; and how, afterwards, you found yourself rather worse off when it did; and, further on, how opulence receded from your grasp the richer you became? If you do not, I can introduce you to a friend who does.

Trade is bad and the American business looks queer. A war and a bad harvest would wind up our clock for a time. Let us hope for the best, and sniff the sweet air that comes across the newly-clad country, for we shall see only a few more such new suits.

Our dog broke his leg and was drowned for it the other day. Caution your dog.

7th May, 1869.—I have no fear for the dear old country. It is young yet. Its strength and progress do not depend on the amusement of the game called Debate. Good things go on growing without the gardeners; and if you parsons keep to the right end of the stick and improve the minds and thoughts of the folks, you will do better than bothering your heads about parliamentarians. Charles the First said the people had nothing to do with the government of a country. Do I not echo the sentiments of the martyr? Let the swells have the seats of sound learning and write all the teaching in newspapers, and make the long speeches—especially after dinner, as in the good old times of Fox and Pitt—and we shall have nothing flimsy or long-winded, and people will learn to respect their betters, and there will be no disestablishment of anything. But you must in that case put down those inclinations to the three R's, which train the common mind to vigorous thought nearly as much as do Greek and Latin, and the mixing of mankind by those infernal machines, the railways, and the daily living history of the world, to be had for one penny, or else you will have these tiresome flimsy writers, and long-winded speechifiers, and bold irreverent low fellows, forgetting their catechism and speaking evil of dignities.

30th August, 1869.—I shall be due at Chester on the 2nd proximo at 9 o'clock, and I propose to present myself to your hospitality on the afternoon of the 1st. I write beforehand in order that the triumphal arches may be prepared and the muslin dresses bought for the twelve Wybunbury damsels who are to strew flowers in my way, from the entrance of the village. Louisa will, of course, fling herself passionately on my neck at the gate of the Vicarage. Kindly give her a hint to take care that I am clear of the steps before she does it; it would spoil all if we both rolled into the road. You and the girls, I suppose, will form a tableau at the doorway during this interesting part of the ceremony. I shall leave your house about quarter to 7 a.m., on the 2nd, to catch the 7.50 train from Crewe to Chester, so that you will be obliged to have the fireworks immediately after the elegant repast in the evening, in order that I may retire to rest early and get some sleep after the serenade. The conjuring by the rural dean can go on while I am partaking of refreshment, just after my arrival; and old Johnson's hornpipe can be done then also. Don't be long, dear friend, in reading the address, but speak the speech, I pray you, "as it were, in a manner of speaking, as the saying is," you know. Let the one volunteer form himself into line in front of the church and commence file-firing from the right, by sub-divisions, on my approach, and then retreat, as his custom is of an afternoon. I presume that on the horsepicious occasion, Cliffe (the horse) will receive two more oats than usual, and the gallant and chivalrous Charles be requested to inspect the inside of a half-pint of beer.

11th September, 1869.—I am on my way back with a sprained knee, got in running last Tuesday: a hint that we "old 'uns" must not come the juvenile, and attempt to run. Doctor—bathings—rubbing—grunts—ah-oh—ah-oh—no end of bother. Every position disagreeable; everybody doing everything the wrong way.

When we find that we can get a few yards with a stick, and make it a matter of congratulation, you may conclude that, physically, there is a screw or a large bolt a little loose, and that our health "aint that sulubrious." My doctor suggested a crutch. Horrid, "yer washup!" Imagine me going to the Committee on a crutch, for promotion, and getting made a full gatekeeper.[1]

13th September, 1869.—After twenty-four years' pleasant steering, here we are,—A1, copper-bottomed, and sea-worthy. We went over Waterloo Bridge together in a cab, and now we have become two bands. Another twenty-four years, and we shall probably have crossed another river—alone,—but the fear of that journey diminishes as age reveals the universal goodness and majesty of God, and the safety of putting our trust in Him. Ages do not complete the revelation of His mysteries, and we may be content with the hem of Christ's garment, to cure our poor complaints.

17th March, 1872.—" And doth not a letter like this make amends for all the long time he's been dreaming away?" said I to myself, when I received yours of the 13th ultimo. Yea, verily, the bottling-up did no harm. The tap is as good as ever; it is laid on from the main, and the turncock isn't within sight. Send me a dozen of the best. I like pleasant things said to me—so keep on saying 'em, like a dear old chap. Indeed, I think the sayer of good things is rewarded as he works at his kindly office. Write you often, and try it. You will be lighter and better for rousing yourself to do it.

28th May, 1872.—We were very sorry indeed to hear of your being ill. The numbness, however, is not, I think, serious. My symptoms of the kind began early in life. I am not such a strongly built time-piece as you, but even you, at length, require winding-up and tinkering. Quiet, quotha! Why, what can be more quiet than lying on your back, in that chair of yours, shut up in your little caboose? Change is the word. Change and careful dieting will bring you right. There is more in this business of regimen than we generally think. Perhaps more Christian virtue, magnanimity, nobility, and great deeds take their rise in what our cook calls the 'stomjack' than in the head or the heart. What is a man without his liver? Go to Leamington, and see. Depend upon it, when we are falling out with our friends, here and there—when our objection to the expenditure in the family gives us a kind of pleasure beyond the actual effect on our purse—when we cast about for a victim to sacrifice to our anger when anything happens wrong, and pitch upon people who are entirely innocent of the occurrence,— then may we place our hand upon our abdomen as the seat of the evil, and appeal to two of Cockle's.

Youth is generous, believes in goodness and purity, takes in the Athanasian Creed, and goes about cheerily, with bright hopes and lots of love for man, woman, and child, and dog— especially Pompey. The 'stomjack' is all right: *vide* suet dumplings, raw chestnuts, green gooseberries, and the like, defied. Let him approach man's zenith—do the hospitality to his friends—pipe to them, and overdo himself in the cause; and you'll find him afterwards remorseful, and sad, and irritable, and bitter; and you may conclude that this is another screw loose in the duodenum, and that the overtaxed gastric department has struck work, on the short hour question.

I thought perhaps it would be agreeable to you all for Bob to turn up to-day. The shadow of evils that *may* befall the home circle—a glimpse of the horse-hair by which the sword is suspended, strengthens old ties of love which may have been growing a little weaker through a long season of prosperity and happiness, sometimes. I don't think any of you want many stimulants to stir up the affection that binds you together. The electric wires are all well laid round you; but some startling evidence of calamity escaped may refresh the battery; and when religion and thankfulness prevail, and the hearts of all are a little softened as yours may all be, the eldest hope is as well amongst you.

5th June, 1872.—How my friends and *confrères* are disappearing, and shunting into retirement,—and how the boys I remember are beginning to assume big places! How distant do early things seem! How many decades of old recollections rise up in my mind—oldest, older, old!—and what was but recently new goes galloping into the venerable and shady past at a speed that startles me often.

I am a farmer, noble sir, on the Grampion Hills, as it were. I bought a cart and harness some twelvemonth ago, and ever since I have been wonderingly gazing upon, or staring at my purchase. I want to know what on earth use it is! A thing of beauty is a joy for ever; but a cart a'int. Hear ye! I am going to sell it—at a loss—at a loss. The rats kill the goslings, and the calf kicks the bucket; the lamb gets caught in a doorway and does for itself; the hens addle the eggs; the horse gets a spavin and is sold—at the precise time that the sow gobbles up nine pigs. Pigeons, also, fall out of their nests and stun their stupid selves; while the young ducks eat all the asparagus.

2nd July, 1872.—Yesterday I steered my little ship round "London's proud city," and to Windsor, and heard part of the evening service in St. George's Chapel—renewed acquaintance with the beautiful monument to the Princess Charlotte, and looked at the monument to Leopold 1st, upon which the Queen has placed an affectionate inscription. Old Windsor looks grey and old. I remember going to see it at the Eton Montem time. Old Cash made the dresses and bags for the boys to beg, "Salt for the Montem, Sir—salt," meaning money for the exhibitioner. The boys were often rude, and some got drunk.

To day it is a pleasure to live. The sun shines, and a pleasant breeze makes a stroll agreeable. I wish I were a parson, with no arguments to use about trade, and rates and trains, and no watchfulness to exercise against competitors—nothing to do but to teach people to be good, and to make visits across green fields to cottages and mansions.

4th February, 1873.—Nuneaton.—The little farm was very pleasurable; it never would have been profitable; but the effect of the long walk through the weather we have had this season on M—— decided me to change at once, and we do feel the advantage of being nearer the station. We are much taken with the snugness of our new place.

We have been greatly shocked at the sudden death of our farm-man Isaac since we left. He was a good-looking, strong, fine young fellow. I sent him as porter to Leamington, and about a week ago he thanked me for the nice place; but he caught a severe cold, which turned to brain-fever and closed his promising young life. His aunt, who keeps a small farm near our old house, bought my best cow, at the sale. The cow was a beauty, but she lately died in calving : a sad loss to the poor body. So the farming ceased gloomily.

One of our managers, a young fellow of thirty-four, died suddenly last week, leaving a wife and seven children, and another on the way ; and my oldest friend on the railway, Mr. Lee, engineer of the Chester and Holyhead District, also died last week. Dark clouds these.

You will perhaps now be little interested to know that the Livock's old house at Hampstead has been cleared away stock and block, and a row of tall houses and shops placed on the site. I am sentimental perhaps, but such changes set me "a-thynkynge, a-thynkynge." The little neat house, the counting-

house door, and the familiar figure at the desk; the cosy parlour
the pretty garden behind the upper floor, the weeping tree, and
the plot of grass, the roses in the summer-time, and all the
figures thereabouts on happy Sunday afternoons; all obliterated.
And of the voices which rang young and clear in the dear old
place, some are still, and the rest are growing thin. It is a long
time ago to recall, and so much has happened since; but the
memory of those days is mellow and sweet.

3rd June, 1874.—The bright, matured, and complete summer
is here—all vegetation teeming with its fullness and beauty. It
is a joy to live at such a time. The meadows, the trees, and the
hawthorn hedges, the sunshine and the soft wind must cheer the
saddest heart, and make the veriest grumbler admit the existence
of some blessings in this life, or, at any rate, *long to be a cow and
wade among the buttercups.*

6th July, 1874.—After dinner I made a wreath of beautiful
roses and carnations for my Amy's grave. She and her two
little ones lie sleeping there; but I think of their dear spirits in
Heaven, with others whom I love to muse about, and whom I shall
soon join—ah, how soon! counting by the speed of dreaming
years which are gone, even if the Master spare me here the full
time.

Pleasant days these happy Sundays! I read the lessons at
Church. Mr. Hands, the son of a late farmer in the neighbourhood, has recently taken orders, and came to read prayers in the
church of his boyhood, for the first time; a comfort, doubtless,
to his poor old invalid mother, our neighbour. Home to supper
and the agreeable hour before bed; and truly, our little service
of Scripture and prayer, at the close of such a day as this, should
be from grateful hearts.

15th July, 1874.—Last night went to see a delightful
historical play called "Clancarty," written from an episode of
William the Third's reign. It is a pity that the stage is not in
all cases true to its mission of teaching elevated thought and
noble aspiration, by good plays; instead of degrading the age
by sensational impurities and indecent spectacle.

31st July, 1874.—Letter from old Mr.———, hinting for a
small sum. Extraordinary old gentleman, that! Clever at making

it appear that he confers a benefit when he asks a loan. He is 86 years old, and walks into———every day from———, and writes a firm, steady handwriting, and lots of it. There has always been something the matter with the Finance Department of his active brain. Always scheming; sometimes with plenty of money; frequently at law; and sometimes in poverty; anon "coming up smiling;" and always alive and kicking, up to 86 years of age. Commercially irregular, if not downright dishonest—yet ever religious, trusting in the providence of God with a coolness that has often staggered me; especially when he has quietly gone into debt, with the full assurance that "God would provide."

4th August, 1874.—Returned last night from a delightful outing to Southampton and Netley, going by way of Leamington, Reading, and Basingstoke. The journey was long, but the weather was bright, and lit up a continued panorama of cornfields, and woods, and shining rivers—the corn, in luxurious abundance, brimming the green-edged basins which held it, like liquid gold; or lying in sheaves at the feet of the triumphant reapers; or standing in serried rank; the proud tall stalks awaiting the gleaming sickle to lay them low. Surely no country presents a fairer face than this England at such a time. The stately woods, bowing their leafy plumes on the hillside, presenting numberless hollows and ravines, suggesting ferns and bluebells and fragrant smells of fallen leaves and scented firs,— and startled game, and cries and whistles from happy birds; the river lying molten in the glowing scene, and the cattle all resigned and placid amidst the heat and flies; white roads marked by lazy teams; spires and hamlets, stately mansions and snug retreats. Happy country.

1st September, 1874.—The busy autumn and winter work has begun on this incessantly labouring Machine of a Railway Night and day, every minute, toil the rapid forces to enable men to run to and fro on the earth. Winter and the late autumn bring endless work to District Managers and all concerned. "Sharpen your cutlass!" as Admiral Napier said when he went to fight the Russians. I must sharpen myself for new duties, although I fear I am getting an old blade and shall not stand the grinding of many more years.

10*th September*, 1874.—Returned home yesterday after a few days' agreeable holiday by the sea, and on the hills, at Borth. Brought my wife a brooch made from the precious stones found on the beach at Aberystwith. Curious that the sea not only invigorates our jaded bodies by the effect of its mysterious iodine, ozone, etc., but casts jewels at our feet as we tread the shingles which fringe its restless waves.

16*th September*, 1874.—I had a strange dream last night. Are these revelations in sleep, which we call dreams, the flickering remains of the early communications with God ?

22*nd September*, 1874.—Another day of beautiful weather and good health. Yesterday most of the home party drove to ———, Lord ———'s noble seat. It seems to be too full of fine paintings and cabinets, and old china, and to have spare rooms, crammed with such valuable things, which are never shown. The family do not appear to occupy the place two months in the year. There is a screw loose in the distribution of these fine things, somewhere.

26*th September*, 1874.—Had a fall over the catch of a turn-table yesterday at Rugby, while running to meet the Chairman. Barked my knee severely, and otherwise shook myself.

28*th September*, 1874.—On Sunday Mr. Baxter, an eminent layman, preached in our Attleboro' schoolroom, before a large congregation. He holds the doctrine of coming to Christ, and immediately receiving the gift of the Holy Spirit, and becoming sons of God, so that we cannot in future fall away, but are saved at once and for evermore. This seems to me too bold a view, seeing that many who entertain it do fall from grace and are guilty of many wickednesses, especially of the sin of want of charity towards their fellow creatures. My humble belief is that we shall always be liable to sin in this present life, and that only in the world to come shall we certainly know what is our eternal destiny. Our part here is to strive against sin, both outward and inward, trusting solely in the merits and atoning work of the Lord Jesus Christ, and in the guidance of the Holy Spirit, for victory now and salvation hereafter; and hoping ever—but not indulging in any overweening confidence, which may degenerate nto vainglory and self-deception.

5*th October*, 1874.—Harvest Thanksgiving in our little church yesterday. No flowers, no corn, or pretty devices in stars, but special lessons and hymns—the latter trolled forth by the strong country voices in gladdening volume, while the words were stirring. We had good and eloquent sermons, both morning and evening, and there was a large collection for the Sunday schools.

17th October, 1874.—Autumn colours come on apace; very beautiful, but very melancholy.

30th October, 1874.—Weather muggy. I notice that in such atmospheres the crop of disputes and differences, domestic and otherwise, is greater than in the fine or bracing weather, when we laugh at small matters. Meanwhile one should keep himself well in hand and treat all these things as a part of the play. It will soon be over; and then for the fresh air and freedom of the better world!

4th November, 1874.—On Monday night, 2nd instant, died Mr. T. Shaw, of the Angel Hotel, Northampton, many years an agent for cartage, etc., at Northampton, and formerly a coach proprietor for the Midland Counties. A kind-hearted, genial, and honest man; always my agreeable and hospitable friend, whom I shall miss very much. One by one, old faces disappear from my circle of friends and acquaintances—bidding me reflect.

24th November, 1874.—Fifty-three years of age yesterday. Many thoughts about that long period: a dream, apparently purposeless. God knows why I was born—what object I have fulfilled. I know nothing: an atom among the myriads of human beings on this globe. More knowledge anon, my friend! A short time more—and then face to face.

PART III.

POEMS.

(I.)

Ever thine,
   Like the sweet woodbine,
   Which doth entwine
The pleasant hedgerows in the summer prime;
   For to this mind of mine
Friendship is fragrance in the lanes of Time.

Always thine,
   At every time;
   In Sol's high prime,
Or when do shine
   The stars which gem the sky;
In winter's wind and snow;
Amid the tints which glow
When Autumn sighs to know
Another year must go;
In summer's flower show,
When silver rivers flow,
And jewelled meadows grow,
And golden sunbeams throw
   Their largess far and high.
Thine in this pleasant spring
With hope in everything,
When birds their wooing sing,
Making the greenwoods ring,
Thine for aye, until we die!
Ever thine,
While life is ours,
And the fleeting hours
   Speed through the glass of Time;
Until Life's weeds and flowers,
And its sweets and sours,
   Cease to be thine or mine.

Yours—still true to you and yours—
While the remaining hours
Gather the weeds and flow'rs
Of this strange life of ours,
And the sustaining Pow'rs
  Guide our poor footsteps to the goal,
Where the sad race is run,
Where all the sorrow's done,
Where, through the Mighty One,
For us the prize is won,
  And Time, for us, will cease to roll.

Yours, my friend,
Till all shall end!
While yet we wend
  Our footsteps o'er Life's chequered way—
  While here we stay—
  We'll shed the ray
  Of Friendship's light, to drive away
  The clouds which darken Autumn's day,
  And so keep old 'dull care' away
  Until we banish him for aye
With purer friendship in the sky.

Yours, while life is ours,
Whether it spits or showers,
  Or rains large cats and dogs—
Blows great guns, or gentle breezes,
Among the chimney-pots and through the 'treeses'—
  In sunshine or in fogs.

Yours always,
While here we 'stays,'
Though Fortune's ways
  May change with us to-morrow;
Beneath the rays
Of summer days,
Or when our gaze
Is dim'd with haze,
  Through wintry winds or sorrow.

SPRING.

Through the mists of dark disheartening winter
With smiling vigour thou dost thrust thy way, O Spring!
Cheeriest daughter of old Father Time, all Nature hails thee,
And in her brightest garb adorns the meadows and the trees.
The young corn creeps through tawny earth and promises abundance;
While the rich grass invites the cattle on a thousand hills.
With mimic snow the hawthorn decks the hedges,
And glowing sunshine paints the flowers anew.

    Spring peeps through wintry clouds
    And calls the timid buds
    To come and dress the woods
      In hopeful green:
    The early flowers hail the sound,
    Creep gently through the melting ground
      And deck the scene.

    The roaring winds—like revellers
    Whom in the night the sleeper hears—
    All die away, and Nature bears
      The soft south breeze a-wooing;
    And tenderly the zephyrs fling
    The breath of life o'er everything;
    And melody, upon the wing,
    Ascends in praise, as birdies sing
      And Spring's green leaves are growing.

    Oh, time of Hope, so sweetly fair,
    In human life or changeful year,
    Ere sorrow's cloud, or stormy fear,
    Or worldly cold, or bursting tear,
    Or treachery's lie, or searching care
      Youth's loveliness hath shorn!
    Stay, fleeting Spring, nor hasten on
    To where so many Springs have flown!
    Life's year, with me, is almost gone;
    The heat and toil are nearly done;
    And I would Nature's youth prolong,
    To cheer me ere I sink among
      My winter thoughts forlorn.

SUMMER.

Nature's great book of Seasons open lies
    At Summer's bright page.
The lark o'er all its beauties gaily flies,
    High in azure cage.

The corn, the kine, the flow'ring meads,
    In sunshine glowing.
The busy insects humming seek their needs
    With joy o'erflowing.

The upland woods soft zephyrs quiver,
    Chasing the light gleams;
And in the vale the glitt'ring river
    Kisses the sunbeams.

All with varied tints and sounds adorn
    Thy Summer pages,
Illuminated book of years unborn
    And bygone ages.

Kindly to man Thy feast is yearly spread,
    The tale repeated.
"Seedtime and harvest," as the Lord hath said,
    In season meted.

While thus I linger o'er thy lovely scenes
    With grateful pleasure,
And drink delight in Summer's waking dreams
    With strolling leisure.

Tell me thy deeper meaning, wondrous teacher,
    While on earth I plod,
Be thou unto my soul a silent preacher,
    Pointing up to God.

AUTUMN.

'Tis Autumn now; and, far and wide,
The bare earth, shorn of cereal beauty,
Yields her rifled bosom to the ruthless plough.
The flowers fade—the swallow quits the scene.
The sighing winds sing dirges sad, to dying leaves,
And whisper tales of winter.
As charms in death the singing of the swan,
The mellow beauty of the coloured woods
Doth shed around a farewell sweetness,
And the swollen stream
Murmurs its sorrow for a summer dead.
Anon the tinted Season, standing on the brink,
Flings her last garment to the prurient winds
And plunges into Winter.
The stars in tearless grief gaze out
Upon her icy coffin and her pall of snow.
The bare ungainly trees wave gaunt and dreary,
Moaning their angry sobs to barren landscapes;
   While Zero sits supreme.

HARVEST.

 Behold the harvest field,
 Adorned with golden yield;
 See how the graceful sheaves
 Embrace in loving wreaths,
  As angels sweet
  Each other greet,
  With bliss complete,
When Peace on Earth, and God's good-will
  To sinful Man are granted.
 Let praise ascend to Heaven
 For bread to mankind given,
 Till thankful harmony shall fill
 The Autumn air, and louder still
  The hymn of joy be chanted!

(IMPROMPTU WRITTEN IN THE VISITORS' BOOK AT THE "HAND" HOTEL AT LLANGOLLEN.)

Romantic Dee upon thy rugged strand
Fair Hospitality extends her "Hand."
Where with wine, ale, or beer,
Or other good cheer,
You've nothing to fear,
Be it cloudy or clear.

The hostess lib'ral and the waitress kind ;
The harper's music fills each passing wind ;
The whisker'd postboy drives a cosy car ;
And all things round and near quite jolly are.

And so 'twill be when I am gone,
This noisy noise will still noise on,
And other folk will cross these bridges,
And try to climb these great high ridges,
For e'en in poverty or riches
Our fleeting life at all time "sich" is.

TO A SUNDIAL.

Thy shadow hand points to the sunny hours,
  But makes no sign for cloudy days or night.
Forget we thus the days when Fortune lours,
  And record only those when she is bright.

BOYHOOD'S HOME.

Oh, can this be the long-loved place,
  The treasured memory of years?
Do my returning footsteps trace
  The home of childhood but with tears?

Tears not of pensive joy, but those
  Which manhood sheds with heaving heart
O'er loved ones lost in death's repose,
  And golden hopes which now depart.

Yon village green, yon house and farm;
  The Holy spire, the purling stream ;
The school-house, scene of dread alarm,
  Recall to mind my boyhood's dream.

But, sad to tell, at any turn
  My gaze meets no remembered face,
And I've come back alas ! to learn,
  On earth there's no abiding place.

HAMPSTEAD.

Dear Hampstead, how I love thy fields,
    Thy verdant hills and prospects fair!
Each pleasant stroll fresh rapture yields,
    With some new scene of beauty rare.

The humble spire amongst the trees,
    Like some sweet violet, half seen,
When by the playful summer breeze
    The leaves are moved which formed its screen.

That modest spire, which gently leads
    The mind "from nature up to God,"
Bears more of Heaven amidst these meads,
    Than temples where the great have trod.

Here have I spent my happiest hours,
    And here my dearest friendships made;
Then doubly dear, like lovers' flow'rs,
    To me is every heath and glade.

If Life's rude tide should bear me far,
    With cruel hand, away from thee,
In memory's sky a leading star,
    Dear Hampstead, thou wilt ever be!

SONG.

How can I marry, Davie dear,
    Although I love so truly?
How can I leave poor sister here
    To pine and die so lonely?

Since her Jamie went to sea,
    And sank beneath the billow,
Her broken heart has clung to me,
    And I have soothed her pillow.

O Davie, Davie, urge no more!
    I dare not listen to thee!
We'll meet again, when life is o'er;
    Here love must yield to duty.

And now the struggle's past, farewell!
    Think of me sometimes kindly;
In twilight musing, when the spell
    Of memory shall bind thee.

A CHRISTMAS CAROL.

(Relating to my family gathering at Christmas, 1866.)

A shepherd I—these sheep of mine
Are on Christ's birthday found
Within my fold—and glories shine
In blessings all around.

For goodness crowning all my days
Which mercy doth afford,
Thy Name to glorify and praise,
My heart inclines, O Lord!

Unto the Saviour lead the way
Of this Thy flock and mine;
Oh, guide us here, Lord, that we may
Join that bright host of Thine!

THREE ACROSTICS.

Music is sweetest in the saddest air;
And pleasure keenest when it follows care.
Riches are holy when they grief remove;
The sharpest anger oft doth friendship prove.
Hatreds are deepest when through love they move;
And Kings are strongest when they rule by love.
The world is full of reconcil'd extremes:
One act distresses and the next redeems.
When Adam fell the gracious Promise came—
New hope to cheer the sorrow and the shame.
So while the rainbow shines on tearful days
Ever should mortals seek Life's cheering rays,
Nor sink beneath Time's brief, though cruel pain:
Dark days but veil the sun—he shines again.

Calm be thy night of slumber, lady fair;
Light be thy resting, till the morning air
And merry sunbeams bring another day,
Restoring health and joy to cheer thy way
And strew thy path with Hope's sweet cheering ray.

Clear brooklets speed to reach the sedgy stream,
Losing their sparkle in the broader tide;
And maidens hasten to life's deeper dream
Regardless of the woes to which they glide.
Avoid the danger, gentle lady fair!
Content gives happiness beyond compare;
Our present joys are best, though they be few.
O'er fancies sigh not, nor for "pastures new."
Keep fast those hopes, you need not fear to rue.

ENIGMA.*

My first is dark, but changes hues
  With moon and stars and weather;
My second unto all is dear,
  And charms the ladies ever.
My whole shapes fair the rudest form;
  By day I'm cool, at night I'm warm.
When I am travelling not, I ride
  Upon the line full often;
A mangled thing I oft become,
  Though not a bone is broken.
E'en when the shades of night descend
  I'm still upon the sleepers;
And yet from home I'm ne'er away
  When morn opes pretty peepers.
In hall and cottage I reside.
When life begins I'm by your side,
And seldom quit though death betide.

* *A Night-dress.*

POEMS WITHOUT RHYME OR METRE.

DEAF.

So sadly still! No sound of voice, no hum of bees, nor song of birds, nor sound of laden cart, nor bark of dog, nor shout of boy, nor clink of gate, nor low of kine. Like funeral plumes, the waving trees sway melancholy; but the murmur of the wind is not to me. I stalk along oppressed, like some sad ghost; and Nature's face, so beautiful to see, wears mocking silence everywhere.

NEW COLLEGE, OXFORD.

I sat within the sacred place, behind men clad in white raiment, who sang praises to God, and I listened to sweet sounds entwined with holy words to stir the soul; and one of those in white said prayers, in tones akin to song, which rang throughout the vaulted space, and lingered, as though angels bore the words away. Then, when from out the throats of stalwart singers burst the harmonious anthem, softened by the melody of youthful voices, and bade the earth be joyful in the Lord, my heart fell down in grateful praise to Him who made all sound and other things of beauty, and I went forth as from a Heaven on earth, stronger and purer for my worldly way.

BRIDAL THOUGHTS.
(L. T.)

She pauses on the threshold of her marriage days, to look once more on that dear place she leaves, and in the sweet recesses of her memory a pensive vision of the happy past she sees. The firelight chat in snug warm winter room. The loving laughter and the tender chide—the words of wisdom and instruction rare, from gifted lips—the pleasant ride—the meadow stroll within the fold of his fond arm who guides her now no more. Paternal love, less passionate than his who claims her now, yet oh! how true. How hard to say, "No more! No more!" Her girlhood gone, a golden light of love sheds beauty on the common things of life which happened in that homely, happy place; and treasured in her heart are all the words of her whose anxious care and never-weary hands tended her growth from infancy till now, sorrowed with her sigh, and loved her smile, and gloried in her hope of wedded joy. Ah me! the chapter's told, and nought remains but recollection; but she prays that God will grant a leaven of the good she learnt beneath her father's roof, and sanctify her new-made home with peace.

Voltaire says that everybody is an anvil or a hammer.
I am content with the patient role of the anvil. Yet a word to the hammer;
It is the regulated stroke which produces the "harmonious blacksmith."
Indiscriminate force may fracture the anvil and destroy its usefulness, as well as the music which sweetens labor.

FURTHER POEMS, &c.
(II.)

As birds unconscious cheer with melody
 At eventide a listening mortal's ear,
So noble deeds in man, with harmony
 Do from his grieved angel chase a tear.

Life is like a sleeper's dream,
A summer cloud, a rippled stream:
But Oh! some dreams are agony;
And clouds with bursting tears we see;
And streams there are seek eagerly
 The bosom of the boundless sea,
 The emblem of Eternity.

The mighty may steal and the multitude plunder,
 And call the dark deed a gilt virtue, all brave;
But the villain who ventures to steal for his hunger
 Must surely be crush'd, the world's morals to save.

CATASTROPHE ON REGENT'S PARK WATER.

A hurrying scene of skating men,
And shouts of glee prevailed, and then
A surging heave, and through the air
Rang screams of panic and despair.
In yawning gulf, or broken square,
Of treacherous ice, the hundreds there
Went down, to strive with death.
The brave held on, with "bated breath,"
And swimmers swam, and down beneath,
With struggles fierce, and gnashing teeth,
Sank those whom aid could ne'er relieve;
While on the fatal water's bank,
With frantic arms and faces blank,
Ran to and fro a helpless band,
With eager minds to help and land
Their friends immersed; but nought to hand
Save trifling means and mocking aid;
And women wept, and some one said,
'Twas "No use risking for the dead."
But bravely plunged some nobler men,
And fought the blocks, brought children in,
And did the hero's work. Ah me!
We sometimes read of, sometimes see
Such horror on the stormy sea;
But never may it fall to me
Again to view such agony.

When the heart by affliction is lowered
   The soul takes its loftiest flight,
As steel shines the brightest when scoured,
   And stars beam the brightest at night.

ROMANS, 12TH CHAP.

Let not conceit e'er whisper thou art wise,
   Crush out the will to spite an evil deed,
Provide things honestly before all eyes,
   Live peaceably, and peace shall be thy meed.

When hunger presses on a fallen foe,
   With unknown hand relieve his bitter need;
Should thirst oppress him, let thine aid o'erflow;
   Thy good be greater, though thy wound still bleed.

WE TWO—DARBY AND JOAN.

The shadows lengthen o'er the lea,
The sunset gleams on tower and tree,
And twilight comes to you and me
In grateful gentle memory.
In youth we shared Life's thoughtless morn
Ere yet to us a care was born,
When Hope and Joy our pathway strewed,
And Love each day some grace renewed;
And time was short, and pleasure long,
And one was fair, and both were strong.
Still hand in hand, when noontide came,
Life's lighter struggles found the flame
Of loving trust burn steadily,
To lighten sorrows cheerily.
Then when the little children's voices
Charmed the home with tender noises,
Cared we, the least, whate'er befel
Our daily lot, so they were well?
Contented, busy, careful time,
Our proud and earnest mid-day prime,
Can we forget the hour of woe,
When deep affliction brought us low,
Or how its fire purified
Our spirits, as the gold is tried?
Ah, No! the darkness might betide,
But soon appeared the silver side,
And bade us cast our grief and fears
On Him who sends or dries our tears.
For children's children round our board,
And "troops of friends" in kind accord,
For peace in our declining days,
And comfort in a thousand ways,
Thy Name, O Lord, we bless and praise!
Of lives so long and richly blest
We humbly leave to Thee the rest.

To ALFRED TENNYSON.

Noble sympathetic spirit,
   Shout thou to future ages Virgil's fame;
And with thy voice harmonious
   Enshrine with his for ever thy fair name.

When vexations press,
And you're feign to confess
That the world is a mess,
And those whom you love
Are as weak as a dove,
Or as mild as, say, cream,
Then think of the nought of it,
Flee from the thought of it,
Change the regime!

THE WIDOW'S PRAYER.

May angels guard my daughter's life,
Her nights from danger and her days from strife;
In heavenward paths may she for ever go,
And taste that peace the world cannot bestow:
So when that He whose hand alone can save
Shall call her mother to the silent grave,
May He, when thus He shall remove
A mother's care, a mother's love,
Guard the lone orphan with His heavenly grace,
And with His love supply a mother's place;
And when to earth her last farewell is given,
May hallowed spirits join our souls in Heaven!

GOLDEN WEDDING.

By the Church and up the Road,
We come upon a white Abode ;—
Orchard and lawn and fount and flowers,
Fish-pond and grounds, and sylvan bowers
Surround the home, where rest and peace
Hold gentle court among the trees ;
And oh ! what lasting memory
Is stored around the red beech tree,
Where bowls and quoits are often play'd
Beneath the ever-welcome shade.
A kindly-hearted couple here
Have dwelt for many a happy year,
And time so tenderly doth lay
His hand on them,—that strange to say
It is their Golden Wedding Day.
  And out of the train,
  Come pouring like rain,
In highest of glee up the steps of the door,
A troop of descendants, some forty or more ;
  The fathers and mothers,
  The sisters and brothers,
The big and the little, the short and the tall,
Yet the jolly Old Homestead has room for them all,
 And while the rooms with kisses ring,
 This is the Song they sweetly sing :—
  We come to hail the day,
  And greet its Golden ray,
  To cheer you on your way,
   Loving kind Parents ;
  To you from whom we sprung,
  For care when we were young,
   We offer Presents.
  In helpless infancy,
  When boys and girls were we,
   Your arms were round us ;
  In youth and maidenhood,
  Your watchful care withstood,
   When evil found us.
  In many an after year,
  Advice and wisdom clear,
  From you were ever near
   To aid and guide us ;

And still at every time,
Your willing voices chime
To help us live and shine,
　　With you beside us.
God bless the Golden Day,
All of us hope and pray,
While, from so far away,
　　Greeting each other
Pray we for happiness
All your green age to bless,
And with our love caress
　　Father and Mother.

THE END.

Not in the pale sick room,
Amidst sad sighs and sorrow,
Wishing the day were night,
Wishing the night were morrow.

Not with the groan of pain,
With nurse however tender,
And leech profound and grave,
May I my soul surrender.

But when some honest work,
By faithful truth and duty,
Drawn to a pleasant end,
Gives to my thoughts a beauty.

Or when with secret sin,
I in remorse have striven,
And some sweet hope within
Assures me I'm forgiven.

Then let the bright shaft speed
Swift to its waiting centre,
Unlock the gates of Life
And bid my spirit enter.

In the year 1890, a terrible domestic calamity befel Mr. Stevenson, and the Directors, "*in recognition of his long and faithful services,*" placed him on the retired list with an ample provision for his declining years.—EDITOR.

Printed in Great Britain
by Amazon